PRAYING GOD'S PROMISES FOR BUSY PEOPLE

PRAYING
GOD'S PROMISES
for BUSY PEOPLE

Len Woods

Tyndale House Publishers, Inc.
Wheaton, Illinois

Visit Tyndale's exciting Web site at www.tyndale.com

Praying God's Promises for Busy People

Designed by Julie Chen

Edited by Susan Taylor

Library of Congress Cataloging-in-Publication Data

Woods, Len.
   Praying God's promises for busy people : Len Woods.
      p. cm.
Includes index.
   ISBN 0-8423-6007-7
   1. Prayer—Biblical teaching. 2. Christian life—Biblical teaching.   I. Title.
BS680.P64 W66 2002
242′.5—dc21   2001007370

Printed in the United States of America

08 07 06 05 04 03 02
7   6   5   4   3   2   1

TO MY FRIEND TOM JONES,
WHO SCOFFS AT THE IDEA OF KEEPING
A PERSONAL PLANNER AND REFUSES TO WEAR A WATCH
YET ALWAYS—*ALWAYS!*—FINDS TIME FOR PEOPLE

PART 2: MIDDAY PROMISES

PART 3: AFTERNOON PROMISES

PART 4: EVENING PROMISES

SPECIAL THANKS GO TO:

JON FARRAR, FOR DREAMING UP THIS PROJECT

AND THINKING OF ME

CINDI, WALTER, AND JACK, FOR PUTTING UP

WITH A HUSBAND AND DAD WHO WAS *TOO BUSY*

LOTS OF MORNINGS AND WEEKENDS, THINKING

AND WRITING ABOUT *THE PITFALLS OF BUSYNESS*

(I *DO* BELIEVE, LORD; HELP MY UNBELIEF!)

SUSAN TAYLOR, FOR ZEROING IN ON ALL THE FIRST-DRAFT FLAWS,

WITH JUST THE RIGHT BALANCE OF GRACE AND TRUTH

MRS. CHARLOTTE ROGERS OF SLIDELL HIGH,

FOR TEACHING A CERTAIN TENTH GRADER HOW TO TYPE

WHY are we so prone to busyness? Well, for starters, a hectic lifestyle seems the obvious path to productivity and—so we believe—fulfillment. (How many successful and important people do you know who sit around all day with nothing to do?) Busyness is also the accepted norm of this generation. I "fit in" better when I am able to compare my crazy schedule with the calendars of my busy friends and neighbors.

We are culturally conditioned to wake up early (and/or stay up late) and to attack our days with a vengeance. We are warriors on a mission: to accomplish more in less time. Our weapons are many: cell phones, Palm Pilots, laptop computers, and overflowing appointment books.

The result is that we feel almost as if we're fighting life. Some days we are able to gloat over small victories—perhaps conquering an especially long to-do list. But most evenings we arrive home battered and exhausted, casualties in a kind of guerrilla warfare against the clock. Too much fast food, commuting, and e-mail. Too many checklists, projects, and meetings—and the sickening realization that we have to do it all again tomorrow! Our weeks are jammed with responsibilities, and our weekends are crammed with activities. When do we rest?

This little book is for those who are tired of hitting the sack every night feeling drained and dry. It's for those who are realiz-

ing that busyness robs them of the richness of life. It's for those who want to know what God says to the stressed-out and overcommitted.

Before we dive in, let me clarify a few things:

First, this book uses the word *promise* not only in the strict sense of a specific divine pledge of what will be but also in the broader sense of a theological truth regarding what is. For example, in devotion 62 the featured "promise" is from Ephesians 1:3, which reads, "How we praise God, the Father of our Lord Jesus Christ, who has blessed us with every spiritual blessing in the heavenly realms because we belong to Christ." Notice that this verse doesn't so much guarantee that God will do something for us in the days and weeks ahead as it reminds us of what God has already done. It is not so much a "promise" (in the technical sense of the term) as it is a reassuring statement of eternal fact—a passage upon which we can stand and be confident.

Second, beware of the common tendency to consider every divine promise or pronouncement (including those made in historically unique situations) as directly applicable to your life. For example, I once knew a well-meaning believer who "felt led by God" to form a Christian sports team, claiming Habakkuk 2:2-3 as a heavenly guarantee that his personal vision would eventually come to pass. It never did—probably because that particular divine promise involved the imminent judgment of Judah some six centuries before Christ, not athletic evangelism in the twentieth century. This Habakkuk passage is not a promise to us, but it does yield a principle for us: God will do what he says. It is imperative for us to look carefully at the context of any so-called promise and compare it with other passages of Scripture before claiming it for our own.

Third, even when we are convinced that a promise or passage applies to our modern-day situation, our attitude must be one of submission to the sovereign plan of God. Our Lord has a divine timetable to which we are not privy. His will for our lives is sometimes inscrutable. He is working for our eternal good, not just our temporal good. Forgetting these truths and having wrong expectations may cause us to completely miss occasions when God quietly makes good on his promises to us. This is a critical point. Recognize the huge difference between (1) grappling with the character and will of God and humbly trusting him to do what he says and (2) the popular "name it and claim it" mind-set that sometimes borders on arrogance and impatience: "I expect God to quickly give me what he has promised!"

When a noted Christian leader was in the late stages of termi-

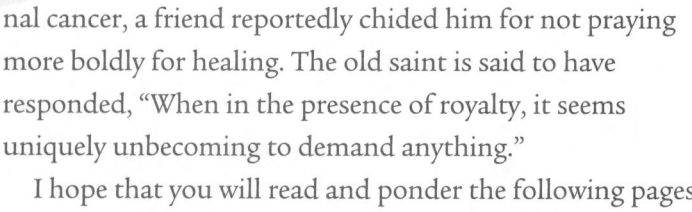

nal cancer, a friend reportedly chided him for not praying more boldly for healing. The old saint is said to have responded, "When in the presence of royalty, it seems uniquely unbecoming to demand anything."

I hope that you will read and ponder the following pages with a trusting heart and not a demanding will. And may God bless you as you do so.

PART ONE

MORNING PROMISES

M ORNING is the time, C. S. Lewis once wrote, when all the thoughts and concerns of the day come rushing at us. Our first obligation is to push them all back and listen to that other larger, quieter voice.

The following thirty promises are helpful in developing a mind-set that resists the lure of busyness by reminding us of the grander truths of God. These are promises to get us started, principles to motivate and inspire, passages to give us the right perspective. It is harder to give ourselves over to trivial concerns when we have a clearer vision of the eternal.

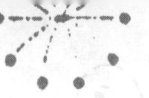
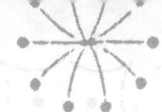
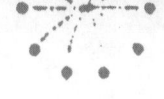

THE PROMISE
GOD HAS CANCELED OUT YOUR SIN

Having chosen [his people], he called them to come to him. And he gave them right standing with himself, and he promised them his glory.

Romans 8:30

SOMEONE has said that religion is spelled *d-o*. In other words, religion consists of all the things we think we have to *do* in order to earn God's approval. The problem with buying in to that idea, of course, is that no matter how religiously we *"do things for God,"* no matter how active we might be in church affairs, we can never know for sure that we've done enough.

Christianity is the antithesis of "religion." Christianity is spelled *d-o-n-e.* Jesus Christ has already accomplished everything necessary for us to experience God's favor. He paid for our sins with his blood. And he offers new life and a right relationship with God as a free gift to all who will stop trusting in their own efforts—what they do—and will trust in him alone.

It's not wrong to be busy serving the Lord unless you think that all your "religious activity" will result in God's favor. You can't earn "right standing." It's a gift.

PRAYING GOD'S PROMISE

Lord, you have chosen me and called me to yourself. I do not understand such love, such grace. But I thank you, Lord. Thank you for saving me from sin. Your Word says that "right standing" with you is a gift. Help me to remember that I cannot earn your approval. Instead, you declare me righteous solely because of what Christ has done for me. If I busy myself in serving you, let it be from a grateful heart and not from a heart that seeks to earn your favor.

GOD'S PROMISE TO YOU

- God chooses his people.
- He gives them right standing with himself.
- He will give them his glory.

THE PROMISE
GOD WANTS YOU TO EXPERIENCE
ABUNDANT LIFE

My purpose is to give life in all its fullness.   John 10:10

JESUS could not have been clearer. He wants us to have the fullest life imaginable. So why do the vast majority of folks settle for a dreary, superficial existence?

Author C. S. Lewis put it this way: "We are half-hearted creatures, fooling about with drink and sex and ambition when infinite joy is offered us, like an ignorant child who wants to go on making mud pies in a slum because he cannot imagine what is meant by the offer of a holiday at the sea. We are far too easily pleased."[1]

Don't be "too easily pleased"! Realize that you were created for so much more than the mindless busyness of a life of "making mud pies." Psalm 16:11 says, "You will show me the way of life, granting me the joy of your presence and the pleasures of living with you forever." Take Jesus up today on his wild offer of joy by seeking to be continually in his presence. The more you are in his presence, the fuller your life will be.

PRAYING GOD'S PROMISE

*You came, Lord Jesus, to give me a full and meaningful life. Forgive
me for the times I settle for a drab, ho-hum life. Forgive me for being
so busy with the stuff of earth that I fail to seek you or even hear
you. Give me the courage to say no to the world's offer of a frantic
life filled with irrelevant activity. Give me a heart that seeks to walk
closely with you.*

GOD'S PROMISE TO YOU

● God wants to give you a rich, satisfying life.

---

[1] C. S. Lewis, *The Weight of Glory and Other Addresses* (New York: Collier Books, Macmillan, 1980),
1–2.

THE PROMISE
GOD IS INTIMATE WITH HIS FOLLOWERS

I no longer call you servants, because a master doesn't confide
in his servants. Now you are my friends, since I have told you
everything the Father told me.   John 15:15

WHEN you think of God, which of his divine roles come to
mind? The Bible describes him variously as creator, sustainer,
provider, father, judge, lord, savior, and king. It also speaks of
him as *friend*.

It's a surprising image, isn't it? Think of it: finite creatures in
intimate and affectionate relationship with an infinite creator!
But the concept is thoroughly biblical. Abraham was called "the
friend of God" (James 2:23). And Jesus referred to his followers
in the promise above as friends.

We need to be careful not to be "flippant" with God or take
our friendship with him for granted. Real friends make the
effort to spend time together on a regular basis—and it never
seems like an effort! The reward of such a relationship is
warmth, love, acceptance, and concern. How are you doing at
cultivating your friendship with God?

PRAYING GOD'S PROMISE

Oh God, you are everything the Bible says you are—creator, sustainer, provider, father, judge, lord, savior, and king. I praise you for being the righteous ruler of the universe—and for making and saving me! But, Lord, you are also my friend. Help me to understand the implications of friendship with you. I want to be loyal, committed, and loving. I want to walk with you daily—and make you smile!

GOD'S PROMISE TO YOU

- You are Jesus' friend.

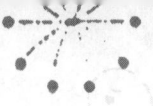
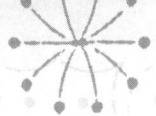

THE PROMISE
GOD'S SPIRIT GIVES YOU INSIGHT

God has actually given us his Spirit (not the world's spirit) so we can know the wonderful things God has freely given us.

1 Corinthians 2:12

WHAT good is an advantage if you don't capitalize on it? What good is a gift you never open?

One of the great gifts God has given Christians is his Spirit, who lives in us. It is the Holy Spirit who imparts the very life of God the Father to us at the time we put our faith in God the Son (Christ). God's Spirit is our counselor (John 14:26). He gives us the ability to live lives that please our heavenly Father (Acts 1:8; Galatians 5:22-23).

But if we are too busy to acknowledge the Spirit's presence or too distracted to listen to his voice, we squander a valuable resource. He longs to direct us down good paths. He wants to show us the deep things of God.

What needs to change in your life—in your schedule—today so that you can pay closer attention to the Spirit's leading? Are you willing to slow down and listen?

PRAYING GOD'S PROMISE

God, you have given me your Holy Spirit. Oh, thank you, Lord! What would I do without your presence in my life? Forgive my foolish habit of not stopping to hear what you are saying, of not asking you to teach me and guide me. Only your Spirit can help me understand all the spiritual blessings I've been given. Teach me to listen to you. Give me ears to hear. There is so much I need to learn about and understand: grace, forgiveness, eternity—you. Keep me from the distractions of busyness, and draw me closer to you.

GOD'S PROMISE TO YOU

- God has given you his Spirit.
- The Holy Spirit will show you the depths of God's blessings.

THE PROMISE
GOD HAS GIVEN YOU ALL YOU NEED
IN CHRIST

In Christ the fullness of God lives in a human body, and you are complete through your union with Christ.   Colossians 2:9-10

THE word *complete* in the verse above means that everything is included or has been done. In other words, nothing else is needed.

In contrast, the word *incomplete* means that something is lacking—and we must either live without that "missing something" or try to acquire it somehow.

How much of our busyness stems from the belief that our lives are "incomplete"? Are we working long hours primarily to acquire things we don't have—and maybe only think we need? Are we playing or vacationing to the point of exhaustion in hopes of acquiring "missing" experiences?

Today's promise says we are complete if we are in union with Christ.

Such a bold statement requires us to ask ourselves: Do we honestly believe Jesus is enough? that he provides ultimate wholeness? that there's no life or meaning to be found outside of him? If we believe those things, maybe we have a solution to our tendency toward busyness.

PRAYING GOD'S PROMISE

Lord Jesus, you are fully divine and fully human. What a mystery! I praise you for becoming a man and living among us. In coming, you showed us what the Father is like. In dying, you offered us the very life of God. I am complete through my union with you! Oh Lord, by grace, through faith, I am eternally linked to you. I am part of your body. I thank you for meeting my real needs fully. Forgive me for the times I think and act as if you are not enough. You are all I need.

GOD'S PROMISE TO YOU

- Christ is fully God.
- You are complete in Christ.

THE PROMISE
GOD HAS FUNDAMENTALLY CHANGED YOU

> Those who become Christians become new persons. They are
> not the same anymore, for the old life is gone. A new life has
> begun!
> 2 Corinthians 5:17

In the pages of this book we're talking about busyness, about how to cope with it and about the ways it can rob us of a rich existence.

Meanwhile life stampedes around us and over us. Urgent demands still scream at us. How unnatural it feels to deliberately go against the flow of the frenetic pace of our culture!

Perhaps as you look at your Day-Timer or Palm Pilot or ponder your own personality and habits, you think, *What's the use? I know that excessive busyness is wrong, but I can't change!*

Let me correct that thinking: You already *are* changed! When God gave you new life (by placing his Spirit within you), a fundamental transformation took place inside you. God replaced the old you with a new nature that has both the desire and the ability to please him. The Christian life is simply the process of working with God to bring that inward change to the surface of your life (Ephesians 2:10; 2 Peter 1:4).

Are you willing today to live out the deep changes that God has already begun in you?

PRAYING GOD'S PROMISE

God, when I first put my faith in you, I became a new person! Thank you for changing me and giving me new life—a rich life that will never end. I am not the person I was—the old me is gone. I praise you because I do not have to keep living the way I used to live. Because of you, I have the capacity to change and grow into the image of Christ. Let others see a stark but attractive difference in me today.

GOD'S PROMISE TO YOU

- In Christ, you are a brand-new person.
- You are not the person you were—your old life is gone.
- God gives his people new life.

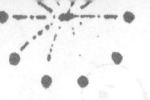

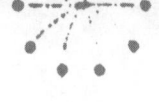

THE PROMISE
GOD FULFILLS YOUR HOLY PASSIONS

Take delight in the Lord, and he will give you your heart's
desires. Psalm 37:4

W HEN Augustine said, "You have made us for yourself, and our
heart is restless until it rests in you," he was referring to the
deepest desires of the soul. Not yearnings for money or sex,
power or pleasure—all temporal thrills that only leave us hungry
for more—but a consuming passion for God and the things of
God.

This is David's point in Psalm 37. God never pledges to
satisfy the superficial longings of our worldly nature. Today's
promise isn't a divine formula for getting that new
extended-cab pickup or the thirty-five-hundred-square-foot
home on the lakefront.

No, to "take delight" in the Lord means to hunger for his
presence, for his will, and for his glory. When God is our
primary focus, our desires change. We find ourselves wanting
what God wants. And that's when we discover our lives being
filled with pleasures that last and truly satisfy.

PRAYING GOD'S PROMISE

God, I want to delight in you. Forgive me for the times I get excited about things that don't matter. I want to enjoy your blessings, but I want to enjoy you and seek you more than anything else. When you become my focus and my passion, I can be sure you will grant the deep desires of my heart. Because I am your child, I know that you've given me a new nature. I'm not the person I used to be. Stir up the holy passions that you've implanted within me so that the things I want most are the things you want most to give me.

GOD'S PROMISE TO YOU

- When your desires are righteous, you can be sure that God will grant them.

THE PROMISE
GOD HAS MADE YOU HIS AMBASSADOR

God was in Christ, reconciling the world to himself, no longer counting people's sins against them. This is the wonderful message he has given us to tell others. We are Christ's ambassadors.   2 Corinthians 5:19-20

GOOD ambassadors lead full lives. They make it their business to understand the culture to which they've been sent. They work at improving their communication skills. They keep up with current events and government initiatives. They host dinners, meet regularly with foreign leaders and embassy colleagues, and serve their fellow citizens who need help while in a distant land. Every day, no matter what's on the schedule, the mission of ambassadors is clear: to serve their government (and host country) with excellence, accuracy, and effectiveness.

This is the Christian's calling too. Our true home is heaven; our King is Jesus. Here in a fallen world our task is to represent Christ and his kingdom, to announce his offer of peace and forgiveness.

The Lord calls us, as his ambassadors, to days full of active, purposeful service but not to days of frantic busyness. Only an eternal perspective about our calling as ambassadors can infuse our daily activities with a sense of mission.

PRAYING GOD'S PROMISE

God, through Christ, you forgive sins and bring sinners back into relationship with yourself. Thank you for drawing me to yourself and saving me. You have given the gospel to me so that I might show it and share it. I'm sorry for the times I've been tight-lipped about my faith. Make me bolder and more winsome to those who don't yet know you. I am your ambassador. Help me to see beyond my busyness today to my real purpose—living for you and representing you. Make me a wonderful example of the blessing that is found in being right with you.

GOD'S PROMISE TO YOU

- Through Christ, God forgives your sin and reconciles you to himself.
- God gives you the good news of the gospel to share with others.
- You are God's ambassador.

8 ⊕ JOB DESCRIPTION

THE PROMISE
GOD'S PRESENCE DRIVES AWAY YOUR FEAR

I command you—be strong and courageous! Do not be afraid
or discouraged. For the Lord your God is with you wherever
you go.   Joshua 1:9

W HEN you make the decision to follow hard after God, your life
will be anything but dull. God will ask you to attempt "impossible" things. He will lead you in and through some dark and
scary situations. Will you feel panicky and uncertain on occasion? Count on it. Will you face discouragement? No question
about it. And meanwhile God will repeatedly call on you to keep
trusting and following where he leads.

Take Joshua, for example. When God tapped him to fill
Moses' sandals and lead the nation of Israel into the Promised
Land, Joshua was uncertain, skittish, fearful—anything but
confident. Recognizing this, God told him four times in eigh-
teen verses, "Be strong and courageous." And then he gave the
reason: "The Lord your God is with you wherever you go."

Where is God leading you? What is he calling you to do?
Whatever it is, no matter how daunting, the promise is this: You
don't have to fear—God is always with you (Matthew 28:20).

PRAYING GOD'S PROMISE

Heavenly Father, your Word speaks of being strong and courageous. You tell me not to be afraid or discouraged. Oh Lord, given my life situation, these commands seem so impossible. I feel the exact opposite of what you are calling me to! You pledge your presence with me everywhere I go. Thank you for this amazing promise. Help me to believe it, not just in my head, but deep within my soul. Make it a bedrock conviction in my life, the kind of truth that brings supernatural peace. I want to live by faith, not by feelings.

GOD'S PROMISE TO YOU

- You do not have to be afraid.
- You do not need to give in to discouragement.
- God is with you everywhere you go.

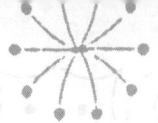

THE PROMISE
GOD LEADS YOU

> You chart the path ahead of me and tell me where to stop and rest. Every moment you know where I am. Psalm 139:3

How common it is for busy people in a busy world to lose their bearings. We sometimes feel disoriented. (*I don't know whether I'm coming or going!*) Occasionally we become discouraged, even despondent. (*I don't understand myself! I don't know how to get off this treadmill!*) At our lowest moments we feel forgotten and alone. (*Can't even one friend or loved one see what a mess I'm in? Everyone is too wrapped up in their own hectic lives to help me.*)

Into our confusion steps the living God with words of assurance. According to the psalmist, he sees us, hears our cries, understands our hearts, knows our situations—everything! He completely understands not only our complicated personalities but also our complex problems. But he doesn't just understand and then leave us to sort it all out for ourselves. He does much more! He pledges to guide us into places of rest. Is there a more comforting promise for people who find themselves caught up in "the rat race"?

PRAYING GOD'S PROMISE

Dear God, you monitor my movements and my thoughts. You always know where I am and exactly how I'm feeling. I want to rest in the truth that I am always on your mind. You promise to guide my steps into places of rest and peace. Thank you for the comfort of knowing that I am known . . . and cared for.

GOD'S PROMISE TO YOU

- God charts your path.
- He will guide you.
- He knows where you are.

THE PROMISE
GOD EQUIPS YOU TO HELP OTHERS

God has given gifts to each of you from his great variety of spiritual gifts. Manage them well so that God's generosity can flow through you. . . . Then God will be given glory in everything through Jesus Christ.   1 Peter 4:10-11

IN Paul's letter to the believers at Philippi he wrote, "Don't be selfish; don't live to make a good impression on others. Be humble, thinking of others as better than yourself. Don't think only about your own affairs, but be interested in others, too, and what they are doing" (Philippians 2:3-4). The picture here is of self-obsessed people who are wrapped up in their own lives from sunup to sundown.

Both of these traits—self-centeredness and busyness—fly in the face of what we're called to be. As Christians, we've been specially equipped by the Spirit of God with supernatural abilities. God means for us to use these gifts to serve others and to accomplish his plan for the world (Ephesians 2:10). When we choose to exercise the gifts we've been given, God gives us the necessary strength, others find needed help, and most important, God gets the glory he deserves.

On the other hand, when we rush around absorbed with our own selfish agendas, everyone loses.

Are you so wrapped up in your own hectic life that others are

missing out on the chance to benefit from your unique, God-given abilities? Take some time to think about whether your agenda is the same as God's agenda. The old saying is true: If you're too busy for people, you're too busy.

PRAYING GOD'S PROMISE

God, thank you for giving me special abilities with which to serve others. Help me to better recognize and understand my gifts. Forgive me for the times I've failed to serve as I could have because I've been too busy focusing on me. Give me an increasing desire to be faithful to my calling. When I make myself available, your power and grace flow through me. I want to be a blessing to others. Most of all, I want you to receive glory. Work in me. Work through me.

GOD'S PROMISE TO YOU

- God gives his people unique gifts and special abilities.
- If you manage them well, God's generosity will flow through you.
- God receives glory when you serve in his strength.

THE PROMISE
GOD HELPS THE WEAK

Those who wait on the Lord will find new strength. They will fly high on wings like eagles. They will run and not grow weary. They will walk and not faint.   Isaiah 40:31

MODERN life has a way of grinding us down. At the end of a hectic day we feel tired. By the end of an activity-filled week, we are dragging. After an extended period of nonstop busyness, we feel physically spent and emotionally wasted. What's the answer for those who find themselves weak of body and weary of soul? "Wait on the Lord."

This rare discipline requires temporarily ceasing your activity (perhaps a half-day retreat or a quiet evening of reflection). It involves analyzing your situation with God's help (talking *and* listening!). Waiting on God *further* involves patience (being still, not watching the clock, focusing on being *with* God rather than on doing *for* God). And finally, waiting involves actively trusting God to meet your need for fresh strength—and all your other needs—in Christ (Philippians 4:19).

The weak soul who "waits on the Lord" becomes a strong soul once again.

PRAYING GOD'S PROMISE

Lord, you promise strength to the weak. I am weak. I sometimes feel that I can't go on. Without your power I cannot live as I should. In you, however, there is new power to fly and run and persevere. I don't want to live a mundane, powerless life; I want to experience your limitless strength so that I can serve you faithfully and be a light for you in a dark world. The only way to experience your strength, God, is to wait on you. Give me the courage to go against the flow of my culture. Teach me the art of stopping regularly, waiting patiently, listening carefully, and drawing fully upon your infinite resources.

GOD'S PROMISE TO YOU

- God will give you strength as you wait on him.
- If you look to God and lean on him you will fly high and run far; you will never run out of power.

THE PROMISE
GOD IS ALWAYS WITH YOU

Be sure of this: I am with you always, even to the end
of the age.   Matthew 28:20

DESPITE a Herculean effort, Susan isn't able to get to the pharmacy, the colleague's surprise birthday dinner, *and* two soccer games between 5:15 and 7:00 P.M. Meanwhile, her husband, Jason, has so much on his "plate" at work and so much on his mind at home that "even when he's there, he's not there."

What is the lesson in this scenario? It is that our busyness typically leads to absence. Which is precisely why it is so helpful to remember today's promise. The truth of that promise is that our busyness does not alter the Lord's *presence* in our lives.

Just before Jesus departed physically from the world, he assured his followers that he would remain with them spiritually in every situation. It's fitting that Matthew concluded his Gospel with Jesus' statement "Be sure of this: I am with you always, even to the end of the age" since he began it by describing Christ as Immanuel, which means "God is with us" (Matthew 1:23).

The next time you feel overwhelmed and alone in an endless sea of obligations, remember that Jesus is with you. He won't ever leave. Will you acknowledge him? lean on him? take the time to enjoy his companionship?

PRAYING GOD'S PROMISE

Lord Jesus, you promised your followers that you would always be with them. Though my busyness often disconnects me from others, it never separates me from you. Lord, this is not just wishful thinking on my part; it's something you said we can "be sure of." I can count on you. Your promise is reliable in a world where most promises are not. Your guarantee is good for as long as I live. Thank you for the permanent nature of your promise.

GOD'S PROMISE TO YOU

- God is with you.
- He will *always* be with you.
- You can be sure of this!

THE PROMISE
GOD GUARDS YOU FROM EVIL

The Lord keeps you from all evil and preserves your life.

Psalm 121:7

In a world that has rebelled against its Creator, bad things *do* happen, and no one is exempt. With such a sobering truth in mind, many spend their lives nervously, busily, and futilely trying to ward off all pain and danger. But the promise above expresses a better, more biblical approach to living in a fallen world.

The verse is from Psalm 121, a hymn of trust that ancient pilgrims often sang on their way to Jerusalem. It expresses the calm confidence that God watches over his people. He has us firmly in his heart and hands.

Of course, this promise is not a guarantee that evil will never touch Christians. (When we read the book of Acts in the New Testament, it's clear that is not the case.) Rather it is an assurance that evil will not ultimately triumph over us (Luke 12:4). We are eternally safe when we belong to Christ (John 10:27-29).

The next time you are frightened by a disturbing news story, rather than expend great time and effort trying to protect yourself, busy yourself remembering that in the Lord you *are* absolutely and eternally safe.

PRAYING GOD'S PROMISE

God, your assurance to your followers is that you will keep them from all evil. Thank you for the knowledge that although evil may come, it has no ultimate power over me. In the words of another Bible promise, "The Spirit who lives in [me] is greater than the spirit who lives in the world" (1 John 4:4). I believe that you will, as promised, preserve my life. I want to live with the confidence that I am safe in you. I am in this world to do your will until you call me home to heaven. Keep me busy trusting, not worrying!

GOD'S PROMISE TO YOU

- God will keep you from evil.
- He will preserve your life.

THE PROMISE
GOD LISTENS TO YOU

The Lord hears his people when they call to him for help. He rescues them from all their troubles.   Psalm 34:17

ONE of the great drawbacks of our busy age is that when life gets overwhelming, it's hard to know where to turn. The reason? Just about everyone else is busy too! Even when you manage somehow to get a friend or family member to sit down and chat, do you really have his or her full attention? Is she truly listening to you or to all the pressures swirling around in her own mind? Is he looking *at* you, or right *through* you?

The biblical promise above is fantastic news to those with heavy hearts, those who have no reliable shoulder to cry on. "The Lord hears his people." Imagine that! The Creator, Almighty God, is *never* too busy to stop and listen to his children. He's a compassionate Father who hears your cries. And he gives you not only his full attention—anytime you need it!—but also the help you need in your time of trouble.

PRAYING GOD'S PROMISE

Oh Lord, you promise to hear your people when they call for help. What a blessing to know that I have access to you, that you listen intently to the deepest cries of my heart, twenty-four hours a day, seven days a week. Not only do you listen, but you pledge to rescue your children from all their troubles. I need you, Lord. I look to you to be my deliverer in every confusing and frightening situation.

GOD'S PROMISE TO YOU

- God hears you when you call.
- He rescues you from trouble.

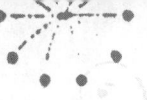
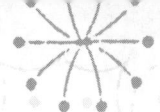

THE PROMISE
GOD HAS SET HIS AFFECTION ON YOU

See how very much our heavenly Father loves us, for he
allows us to be called his children, and we really are!

1 John 3:1

WHAT does success look like? Put another way, what drives *you*
to excessive busyness? A close, happy family? An important,
well-paying, or fulfilling job? Good looks? Material wealth? A
set of faithful friends? Athletic or artistic achievement? Something else?

Many Christians busy themselves in the pursuit of one or
more of these often elusive goals, all the while forgetting that
they already possess life's most precious treasure.

According to the promise above, Christians are already loved
and accepted—fully and completely (Romans 5:8). When we
trust in Jesus to forgive our sins, our status before God changes
instantly. We stop being his enemies and become his friends
(Romans 5:10). Better than that, we actually become God's
beloved children (John 1:12)! He adopts us into his family
(Romans 8:15) and makes us his heirs (Galatians 3:29)!

The next time you're tempted to feel insignificant, think
about how amazing it is to be God's child!

PRAYING GOD'S PROMISE

Lord, even though you are the Holy One, the Creator of the universe, the God who sits enthroned above the heavens, you actually love me! I praise you, Father! Your love is not mere wishful thinking on my part; it is a heavenly fact. The Cross is the proof of that. Help me to appreciate your love even though I will never fully comprehend it. Thank you for adopting me into your family. I am not just a forgiven sinner. I am your child because of what Christ has done. Help me today to live out my true identity. Help me to model your love for those who still have not experienced it.

GOD'S PROMISE TO YOU

- God loves you.
- He has made you his child.

THE PROMISE
GOD BLESSES YOU WHEN YOU WORSHIP HIM

There is really only one thing worth being concerned about.
Mary has discovered it—and I won't take it away from her.

Luke 10:42

How easy it is to fall into the trap of thinking that God is primarily interested in our spiritual activity: helping this person, serving on that committee, leading this Bible study, assisting with that church project. All of these things may be important, but God wants us to be *with* him more than he wants us to do things *for* him.

When Jesus showed up at her door, Martha rushed into the kitchen and began frantically to whip up a world-class feast. Mary, on the other hand, stopped everything she was doing and parked herself in the living room at Jesus' feet. She lingered in his presence, listening to him, enjoying him, adoring him.

When Martha got irritated at her sister, Jesus gently rebuked Martha. Then he praised Mary for her priorities.

What about you? Is your tendency to work first or worship first? According to Christ, our top concern should be to focus on him. When we do, we find a blessing that will never be taken away.

PRAYING GOD'S PROMISE

Lord, our task-oriented world tends to view "get it done" people like Martha in highest regard. And sometimes I buy into this kind of thinking—that spiritual busyness is next to godliness. But you hold Mary up as a model of following you. The top priority, the one you want to see in each of your people, is a heart that longs to be with you. Change me, Lord. I know you want me to use my gifts to serve you and others, but before I do that, Lord, you want me to spend time in your presence, getting to know you, giving you the attention and the affection you deserve. Help me to make that my first priority.

GOD'S PROMISE TO YOU

● God will bless you as you love and worship him.

THE PROMISE
GOD'S WORD KEEPS YOU FROM SIN

How can a young person stay pure? By obeying your word and following its rules. . . . I have hidden your word in my heart, that I might not sin against you.   Psalm 119:9-11

TAKE a day loaded with responsibilities, a day when we're "on the go," trying feverishly to get a hundred and one things done. Did you know that that's a day when we are highly vulnerable to sin?

Why? Because on those days we become task-oriented, embracing a clear agenda with definite objectives. That's not necessarily a problem—*unless* (perhaps *until* is a better word!) someone or something blocks our path in accomplishing our goals. Suddenly we get irritated. We fume at other drivers. Criticize colleagues. Snap at salesclerks. In short, we leave a trail of human devastation all around us.

Today's promise shows a way around this common scenario. We must take God's Word seriously. We must read it, memorize it, and think about it all during our busy days. We must let Scripture shape the way we think and alter the way we act. It's only as we do this that we will live a pure life that honors God. Do you hide God's Word in your heart?

PRAYING GOD'S PROMISE

God, your Word says that living a pure life is possible. I know I'll never be perfect in this life, but I do want to live in a way that honors you. If I hide your Word in my heart, I can keep from sin! Grant me the wisdom to seek you, the discipline to get into your Word (and to get your Word into me!), and the discernment to apply your truth to everyday situations. Keep me from evil, God, for you deserve to be served by people who have pure hearts.

GOD'S PROMISE TO YOU

- God has given you his Word.
- Hiding God's Word in your heart will keep you from wrong attitudes and actions.

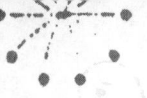
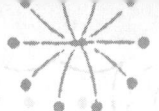
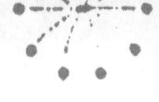

THE PROMISE
GOD HAS MADE YOU HIS HEIR

> [God's] Holy Spirit speaks to us deep in our hearts and tells us that we are God's children. And since we are his children, we will share his treasures—for everything God gives to his Son, Christ, is ours, too.
>
> Romans 8:16-17

THEY were wealthy, middle-aged, and childless. So they did what lots of couples do. They adopted a child to love and care for. When they died, their son inherited everything—a hundred million dollars in assets. What had the boy done to deserve such an inheritance? Nothing. The parents chose him. *They* adopted him.

This true story is analogous to what God has done for us. He chose us. He reached out to us. He forgave our sin. He brought us into his family. It was all *his* decision. We had nothing to do with any of it, except to respond in stunned faith after God had already done everything that was necessary.

Oh, and did we mention the infinite, eternal inheritance? That's ours too. *All* of it. So when we're tempted to spend every waking hour working to accomplish the things on our to-do list or putting in overtime to be able to purchase things that we want but don't really need, we need to ponder these important truths. What do they have to say to overly busy Christians? How can grasping those truths help to alter your mind-set about what's really important?

PRAYING GOD'S PROMISE

Your Spirit, God, reminds me that I am your child. I will never know why you chose me, why you loved me and adopted me into your family. But I am grateful. I praise you. I thank you with all my heart. As your child I am your heir. All that you have is mine! It is hard to comprehend such a breathtaking promise, but the fact is that I am wealthy beyond words! Make this life-changing truth more than "head knowledge" to me. Cause it to sink deeply into my soul and alter the way I live on a daily basis.

GOD'S PROMISE TO YOU

- The Holy Spirit tells you that you are God's child.
- As God's child, you will share *all* of his treasures.

THE PROMISE
GOD ALLOWS YOU TO GO THROUGH HARD TIMES

If we are to share his glory, we must also share his suffering.
Romans 8:17

W HAT words are starry-eyed lovers usually focusing on when they repeat their wedding vows? "To *have* and to *hold* from this day forward, for *better* (for worse), for *richer* (for poorer), (in sickness) and in *health,* to *love* and to *cherish* (till death do us part)." Do you notice how the focus seems to be on the positive aspects of life together? When we think about it, most of us realize that in this world we have to take the bad with the good. But we sure don't like to think about hard times, much less live through them.

What's true in marriage is also true in following Christ. In the previous devotion we looked at the promise that believers in Jesus get all the riches of God. Talk about exciting! Today's promise—from the very same passage—is more sobering: Being a child of God also means suffering (John 15:20; Colossians 1:24; 2 Timothy 3:12; 1 Peter 4:12).

There are no simple explanations for this hard reality. But God's Word does guarantee that trials don't last forever (Psalm 30:5) and that on the other side of suffering is glory (2 Corinthians 4:16-18). Staying focused on these truths during tough times is a good kind of "mental busyness" that pays long-term dividends.

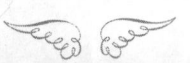

PRAYING GOD'S PROMISE

Lord, I love to think about your promise of glory! One day I will be with you. I will see you as you are. I will share in the great inheritance that you have promised to all your children. But the other side of that promise says that before I share in your glory, I must share in your suffering. Father, I don't like to think about that part of the promise. Suffering is confusing, painful, and something I try desperately to avoid. When hard times come, help me to respond in a godly way. Keep me from complaining. Use the difficult times in my life to mold me into the person you created me to be.

GOD'S PROMISE TO YOU

- One day you will share Christ's glory.
- Before you do that, you must share his suffering.

THE PROMISE
GOD HONORS YOUR FAITH

You see, it is impossible to please God without faith. Anyone who wants to come to him must believe that there is a God and that he rewards those who sincerely seek him.

Hebrews 11:6

BUSYNESS and faith are uneasy neighbors.

Busyness says, "Don't just stand there! Get busy! Get moving! Do something! Rush! Go! Now! Quick! Work! Press! Push! Hurry! Finish! More! More! More!"

In contrast, faith says, "Don't just 'do something.' Stand and wait. Be quiet. Be still. Seek. Listen. Trust. Obey. Go against the flow."

Our world prizes busyness. Who gets praised and promoted? Lots of times it's the person with the fullest Day-Timer, the one who logs the most hours at the office.

God, on the other hand, values faith. The Bible says that without deep trust in the invisible realities of life, we'll never encounter the living God or experience the incomparable blessings he wants to give us. God rewards those who sincerely seek him.

And at the end of the day, isn't that the kind of reward we really want?

PRAYING GOD'S PROMISE

Without faith, God, I cannot please you. Forgive me for the times I wrongly imagine that a busy life is the way to fulfillment. Real faith believes that you, the God of the Bible, are the one true God. Lord, deepen my trust in you. Reveal yourself to me in new ways. I demonstrate true faith by seeking after you, and when I do, you reward me richly. Give me a heart that is sincere. Give me a faith that is persistent, that never stops pursuing you. Finding you is the great hope of my soul and the greatest reward I can imagine.

GOD'S PROMISE TO YOU

- You cannot please God apart from faith.
- He will reward you if you seek hard after him.

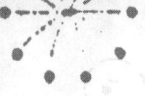
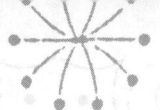
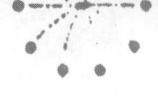
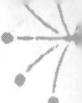

THE PROMISE
GOD'S WORD POINTS THE WAY TO SUCCESS

Study this Book of the Law continually. Meditate on it day and night so you may be sure to obey all that is written in it. Only then will you succeed.   Joshua 1:8

IT'S the same scene every weekend. Tens of thousands of people pack convention centers and hotel ballrooms across the country to hear self-help gurus, motivational speakers, and financial experts speak on how to be successful. Most of these events are slick and entertaining. And many of the people who attend come away feeling motivated and helped, caught up in the possibility of "realizing their potential" or "seeing their dreams become a reality." But how much of the advice they hear really squares with what God has said about how to succeed?

According to today's verse, true success isn't about making money, practicing positive thinking, or getting people to do what you want. On the contrary, God defines success as knowing and obeying what his Word says. We achieve lasting glory—true success—when our sole goal is to honor the Lord.

PRAYING GOD'S PROMISE

You have given me your Word, Lord. Thank you for revealing yourself and for showing me the right and best way to live. True success requires that I immerse myself in your Word and submit to what it says. I cannot please you or find fulfillment unless my life is solidly built on your truth. Give me the discipline to study the Scriptures, the desire to meditate on them, and the courage to obey what they say.

GOD'S PROMISE TO YOU

- If you study and meditate on and obey God's Word, you will have true success.

THE PROMISE
GOD PROVIDES A SOLUTION FOR
HARRIED SAINTS

The Sovereign Lord, the Holy One of Israel, says, "Only in returning to me and waiting for me will you be saved. In quietness and confidence is your strength."   Isaiah 30:15

I t was George Santayana who observed, "Those who cannot remember the past are condemned to repeat it." This is precisely the reason the church (i.e., the modern-day people of God) would be wise to ponder carefully the experience of the Jews in the Old Testament.

By the time Isaiah arrived on the scene in 739 B.C., Israel had split into two separate kingdoms. Like the ten tribes of Israel to the north, the two southern tribes, Judah and Benjamin, had forgotten God and were beginning to experience the consequences—life apart from his blessing. Isaiah urged them to turn around . . . or else.

The details may vary, but the principles and promise are still valid today. To experience all that God wants for you, you must turn to him, wait for him—and walk with him—in quiet trust. If you forget him or, worse, turn away from him, you do so at your own peril.

PRAYING GOD'S PROMISE

Lord, you are sovereign and holy. Forgive me for acting as if I am in charge of my own life and for doing unholy things. Blessing and strength are mine only when I quietly trust in you. God, I want to live a rich, full, satisfying life, one that pleases you and keeps me close to you. Give me the wisdom to see such an existence is possible only when I look to you and wait for you. Even if everyone else is busily going in another direction, give me the courage to seek after you.

GOD'S PROMISE TO YOU

- When you return to God and wait for him, he will deliver you.
- You will find strength when you quietly trust him.

THE PROMISE
GOD HONORS HIS FAITHFUL SERVANTS

Those who love their life in this world will lose it. Those who despise their life in this world will keep it for eternal life. All those who want to be my disciples must come and follow me, because my servants must be where I am. And if they follow me, the Father will honor them.   John 12:25-26

Look carefully at each of the verbs in today's promise passage: *Love. Lose. Despise. Keep. Want. Come. Follow. Be. Honor.* These are meaty words with serious implications.

The truth is that those who opt for a petty, self-absorbed existence will miss God and the eternal blessings he offers. In other words, they will miss out on true life. On the other hand, those who exchange their self-centered, temporal agendas for Christ's will see the deepest desires of their hearts fulfilled in ways they cannot imagine; that is, they will keep, or discover, real life.

So . . . are you following Christ, wanting his will above all else? Are you embracing his attitudes and values, coming to him and following where he leads? Are you making Christ foremost in your thoughts and actions? Are you being with him and following him . . . at home, in your neighborhood, and in your workplace? That is what his servants must do. If you are, the payoff is this: God promises to honor you in heaven!

PRAYING GOD'S PROMISE

Lord, your Word says that those who love their lives will lose them in the end and those who despise their lives will find true life, life that never ends. Thank you for saving me, for showing me that you and your glory are the point. I am not. You are worthy of all that I am—my attention, my affection, my adoration, my life. You bid me to come and follow, and as I do, I will find your honor. How easy it is, Lord, to forget my purpose, to forget that I was made by you and for you. Give me the discernment and the courage to pursue you above all else. You alone have the words of eternal life.

GOD'S PROMISE TO YOU

- God blesses those who give their lives away.
- God honors those who follow Christ.

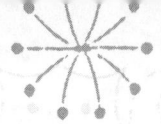

THE PROMISE
GOD'S SPIRIT INSTRUCTS YOU

I advise you to live according to your new life in the Holy Spirit. Then you won't be doing what your sinful nature craves. . . . The Spirit gives us desires that are opposite from what the sinful nature desires.   Galatians 5:16-17

Do you ever stop to think about how often we seek counsel? Engaged couples (wise ones, anyway) pursue premarital advice and counseling. People with money woes make appointments with financial planners to gain wisdom on how to handle their finances. Businesses routinely hire consultants. Let's face it—getting good guidance is a smart way to either get out of trouble or stay out of trouble.

This is equally true in the spiritual realm. God has given us his Spirit to be our permanent, resident Counselor (John 14:26). The Holy Spirit not only shows us which direction to go, but he also gives us the power to live as we should. He teaches us not to give in to sinful desires, and he gives us desires that are in line with what God wants for us.

Today as you interact with others and immerse yourself in a full schedule, listen to the quiet voice of the Spirit. He is a perfectly wise counselor who longs to show you the best course of action in each situation.

PRAYING GOD'S PROMISE

I have a new life in the Holy Spirit. Thank you, God, for coming to live inside me so that I might have the benefit of your continual counsel. Keep me from doing what my sinful nature craves. Make me more desirous of following the leading of the Holy Spirit.

GOD'S PROMISE TO YOU

- God has given you his Spirit.
- As you listen to the Spirit's counsel, you will live as you should.

THE PROMISE
GOD SATISFIES YOUR DEEPEST LONGINGS

[Jesus said,] "The water I give . . . takes away thirst altogether. It becomes a perpetual spring within them, giving . . .
eternal life."   John 4:14

MARK Twain once observed, "You don't know quite what it is
you want, but it just fairly makes your heart ache, you want it
so." It's a shame the great humorist never took to heart the
words of Augustine that we read in devotion 7.

The fact of the matter is that we are restless, aching, hungry,
thirsty people. Look around you. Look at the myriad ways
people try to fill the gnawing emptiness inside them. This frantic soul-searching helps explain much of our compulsive busyness. We're always on the hunt for something that will once and
for all satisfy us and fill us and quench our thirst.

Ultimately only one Person can do that. If your heart is
parched and your soul is thirsty, you need to know that Jesus
offers the living water of salvation . . . to you and to all who will
come to him in simple faith. If you have never drunk from the
living water that Christ gives, go to him today, and ask him to
be your Savior and give you new life.

PRAYING GOD'S PROMISE

Jesus, you are the only one who can satisfy my deepest longings. Remind me that nothing in a temporal world can bring lasting fulfillment to an immortal soul. The life that you give is my internal source of continual refreshment. Teach me the holy habit of looking to you alone for whatever my soul needs. Keep me from believing that physical things can gratify spiritual desires.

GOD'S PROMISE TO YOU

- God alone can quench your spiritual thirst.
- He gives you eternal life.

THE PROMISE
GOD SETS YOU FREE IN CHRIST

You are not slaves; you are free. But your freedom is not an excuse to do evil. You are free to live as God's slaves.

1 Peter 2:16

THE Bible says that Christ came to set us free (John 8:36)—*wonderfully* free from sin's horrible penalty and its terrible power. *Gloriously* free from guilt and shame. *Marvelously* free from a life of empty religious drudgery.

But if you look around you (and maybe even within you), you don't always see the glad signs of freedom. You see Christians trapped in unhealthy habits and destructive lifestyles. You see exhausted believers who view the Christian life as an oppressive list of dos and don'ts.

Christ came to set us free. Free to enjoy the rich banquet of endless grace. Free to throw back our heads and laugh at the wonder of having our sins forgiven. Free to give ourselves fully to the task for which we were created, the only task that can fill our hearts—serving our gracious God.

Are you living like the free person you are? Spend some time today rejoicing in the freedom God gives us in Christ.

PRAYING GOD'S PROMISE

I am truly free in Christ. Lord, this is a phenomenal truth! But it's a sad truth that I do not always live it out. Instead of joyfully delighting in your refreshing "pool of salvation," I often feel as if I'm grimly dog-paddling, just trying to keep my head above water. The truth is, I am free, not to live as I want, but to live as you desire. Teach me to believe the paradox that I am most free when I am living as your servant. Help me to better understand grace, and free me from the curse of a life filled with busyness.

GOD'S PROMISE TO YOU

- God has set you free in Christ.
- You will experience true freedom when you serve him in grace.

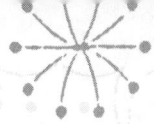

THE PROMISE
GOD GIVES HIS CHILDREN UNEARTHLY
HAPPINESS

I have loved you even as the Father has loved me. Remain in
my love. When you obey me, you remain in my love, just as I
obey my Father and remain in his love. I have told you this so
that you will be filled with my joy. Yes, your joy will overflow!

John 15:9-11

IT'S a pretty grim world out there, don't you think? Grouchy,
grinchy neighbors. Dour, sour coworkers. Journalistic purveyors
of doom and gloom.

Now, in contrast to this joyless existence, think about the life
Jesus has in mind for the children of God. Christ wants his
followers to be secure in the Father's love and therefore "filled"
with joy. It's a joy so immense that it "overflows" our lives and
has an impact on others.

This is not worldly giddiness or silliness. It's not "happiness"
that depends on good circumstances. It's not whistling in the
dark or ignoring the difficult times we may be going through.
Rather, the joy Jesus promises transcends our difficulties. It is a
supernatural sense of well-being that comes from knowing
God. It is the bedrock confidence of soul that all is well because
God is indescribably good.

We find that overflowing joy when we obediently immerse
ourselves in the depths of God's love.

PRAYING GOD'S PROMISE

You want me to know your love, Lord. I experience that love as I obey you. Teach me the great truth that the safest and most wonderful place on earth is with you. You want me to overflow with joy. God, make my eyes dance with joy. Put a spring in my step. Fill my soul with delight as I seek you and obey you and taste your goodness. Make me attractive to those trapped in joyless lives, and let the joy you give me overflow to them.

GOD'S PROMISE TO YOU

- God loves you.
- You experience God's love when you obey his will.
- God's love results in true overflowing joy.

THE PROMISE
GOD CONTROLS EVERY SITUATION

Do not forget the things I have done throughout history. For I am God—I alone! I am God, and there is no one else like me. Only I can tell you what is going to happen even before it happens. Everything I plan will come to pass, for I do whatever I wish.   Isaiah 46:9-10

WE love feeling "on top of things," that we are "in command" of our life situation. We loathe feeling that we are not "in control."

But in reality, control is only an illusion. We can't script our days any more than we can plan out next week's weather. The truth is that life throws curveballs. People act and react in unexpected ways. Each new day brings surprises, interruptions, and events that weren't in our plans. You would think that we'd catch on to the fact that we're mere mortals and that we actually control very little. But we don't seem to learn that lesson very well. We may sincerely give up a situation to God for a while, and then, before we know it, we've tried to take control back again.

The promise above is a good reminder for those times when our plans don't work out. It tells us that God is God—we are not!—and that *he* is in control! Coupling that truth with the fact that God is good is the first step to finding peace in busy, tense, or unexpected situations.

PRAYING GOD'S PROMISE

Your fingerprints, Lord, are all over human history. Thank you for being in control not only of my life but of the whole world. You alone know the future and can orchestrate the events of life. Keep me from foolishly believing that I can control the outcome of my own plans. Give me the grace to trust that you know best and that you will work for my good and your glory.

GOD'S PROMISE TO YOU

- God is God.
- He is in charge of what happens in history.
- His plans for the future cannot be thwarted.

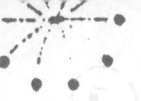
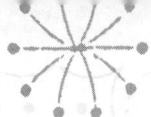
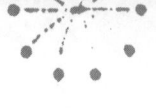

THE PROMISE
GOD USES PURE PEOPLE

> If you keep yourself pure, you will be a utensil God can use for his purpose. Your life will be clean, and you will be ready for the Master to use you for every good work. 2 Timothy 2:21

It has been said that every person longs for two things—relationship and impact. God created us to connect with him and with others; he also created us to make a difference in the world. No wonder we want to do something lasting and significant with our lives.

The promise above weaves together these two longings. It tells us that if we are relating rightly to God by keeping ourselves pure, then he will use us to do important things to fulfill his purpose in this world.

Take some time to reflect on your own life. Is God using you? If not, it might be because of disobedience. Would you knowingly drink out of a dirty glass? Neither will God choose to use a believer who is harboring unconfessed sin in his or her heart.

Admitting our sin and thanking God for his forgiveness is the way we find and receive ongoing cleansing (1 John 1:9). That's the necessary first step for becoming a powerful utensil in the hands of God.

PRAYING GOD'S PROMISE

You want to use me for your purposes, God. Thank you for allowing me to participate in your eternal plan. Only if I am pure and clean will I be a utensil that is useful to you. Show me any failures or wrong choices that I need to see, admit, and turn from. I want to be clean. I want you to use me for your good works. Please make me an instrument you can use to fulfill your purpose for me and for the world around me.

GOD'S PROMISE TO YOU

- God wants to use you.
- If you are pure, he will use you to accomplish his purposes.

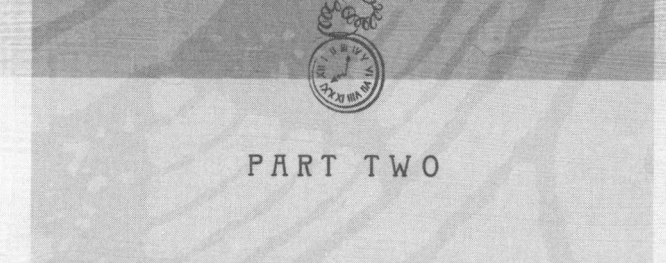

PART TWO

MIDDAY PROMISES

T H E middle of the day gives us the opportunity to catch our breath. Perhaps the morning hasn't unfolded as we imagined. Maybe we've encountered negative situations or people and we're beginning to feel the first twinges of panic about how the rest of the day will go. The noon hour can serve as a kind of oasis—a chance to step back, refresh ourselves, regain our bearings, and find the strength we need to be able to continue.

The next thirty promises for busy people can motivate us to stay calm and keep doing right—no matter what unfolds.

THE PROMISE
GOD IS GOOD

The Lord is good. When trouble comes, he is a strong refuge. And he knows everyone who trusts in him. Nahum 1:7

S OMEONE once said that the great struggle in life is believing that God is good.

In the Garden of Eden, Adam and Eve doubted the goodness of God—apparently thinking that he was withholding something wonderful from them. As a result they chose to disobey God and sample the forbidden fruit, a decision that plunged the entire human race into sin.

We are not different from Adam and Eve. We wrestle with the same old doubts about God. Why else would we refuse to do what a good God says—or choose to do the very things he forbids because he knows they are not good for us? When trouble comes, do we run to God for refuge, or do we run from him and try to solve our problems on our own, believing that if God really loved us, he wouldn't have allowed this thing, whatever it is, to happen to us?

The truth you must take to heart today is that God *is* good. So are his plans and purposes for you. He wants only the best for those he loves. Ask him to make that truth real to you today.

PRAYING GOD'S PROMISE

Your Word says that you are absolutely good, Lord. Teach me to trust wholeheartedly in this most basic of truths. When I am in trouble, I can run to you, experience your goodness, and find you a strong refuge. Keep me from the foolish mistake of believing that I can find life and help outside of you. Thank you for loving me, for watching over me, for knowing me and all my needs. Open my eyes to your goodness, and help me to trust in it.

GOD'S PROMISE TO YOU

- God is good.
- He is a strong refuge in trouble.
- He intimately knows those who trust in him.

THE PROMISE
GOD IS YOUR SHEPHERD

The Lord is my shepherd; I have everything I need.   Psalm 23:1

PSALM 23 is arguably the most beloved chapter in the Bible. And for good reason. It contains beautiful imagery of God's care and concern for his people.

In David's picture we are sheep. The implication is that we are helpless, not too bright, skittish, and prone to wander off and get into trouble. For many of us, that's a fairly accurate description of an average day!

The Lord, however, is called our shepherd (see also John 10:11-15). He is depicted as watching over us, leading us, feeding us, protecting us, and caring for us. As long as we stay close to him, we have no worries whatsoever.

If the Lord is our shepherd, we have everything we need. That's the timeless message of the Bible's most famous psalm. Can you think of any promise more relevant for busy Christians in a bustling age?

PRAYING GOD'S PROMISE

Shepherd of my soul, I praise you and thank you for your care! You are not just my creator or my God. You are not just the king or the judge of the universe. You are my shepherd. I am so blessed! Because of you, I lack nothing. Lord, keep me from complaining. Help me not to worry. Let me rest in the promise that as I go where you lead, you will meet all my needs.

GOD'S PROMISE TO YOU

- The Lord is your shepherd.
- He will provide all that you need.

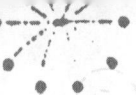
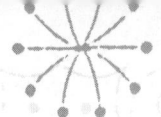

THE PROMISE
GOD IS YOUR FATHER

To all who believed him and accepted him, he gave the right to become children of God.   John 1:12

In the classic Christmas movie *It's a Wonderful Life* a delivery boy named George Bailey is told to take some diphtheria medicine to the Blaine family. But George hesitates. He's pretty sure the druggist, despondent over the death of his own son, has inadvertently put poison powder in the capsules. Frozen in indecision, George looks up to see a sign on the wall advertising Sweet Caporals cigarettes. The sign reads simply "Ask Dad. He Knows." With that, George grabs the box of pills and dashes out the door to his father's office.

What a great picture of the privilege we have as Christians! When we acknowledge Christ as our Savior, he not only forgives our sin but he makes us *children of God.* This means that in the confusing busyness of everyday life, we have a perfect Father who is always glad to guide us. We have the awesome privilege of asking our heavenly Father for help anytime we're uncertain about what to do. He knows the answers to our questions, and he's always available when we run to him.

PRAYING GOD'S PROMISE

Lord Jesus, I do believe in you. Thank you for revealing yourself to me. I have trusted you as my Savior and Lord. Thank you for saving me! Because of your grace and my faith in you, I am a child of the living God. What a privilege! What joy to know that in every situation I have a loving, wise, and good heavenly Father who is always available to counsel me.

GOD'S PROMISE TO YOU

- You are God's child if you believe in and trust his Son.

THE PROMISE
GOD IS YOUR PLACE OF SHELTER

The Lord is a shelter for the oppressed, a refuge in times
of trouble.   Psalm 9:9

EVERY action movie worth its weight in popcorn features some
kind of chase. An evil villain or some ominous fate threatens the
main character, and he or she is trying to make it to safety.
Therein lies the tension.

Of course, most movies are overly simplistic and predictable.
It's fairly clear from the start who the "bad guys" are, and we're
pretty sure that everything will turn out fine by the end of the
movie. Life, on the other hand, is not so predictable. Our
enemies don't always come dressed in black and speaking with
foreign accents. We don't have stunt doubles to leap from
balconies for us or to take the kicks and punches that life in a
fallen world brings. We don't have the luxury of reshooting
when we flub a scene.

What we *do* have for our moments of uncertainty and fear
and panic is the sure promise that God is our refuge and place
of shelter in the storms of life. He is the one to whom we can
run. And when we do, we find safety, peace, and rest in him.

74

PRAYING GOD'S PROMISE

Lord, sometimes I do feel oppressed by life, by concerns and worries and complicated situations. Help me to remember that you are a shelter for those who are weary and afraid. You are my refuge in times of trouble. I thank you for friends, family, and material blessings, but what I really need is you. Thank you for always being there when I run to you.

GOD'S PROMISE TO YOU

- God is a shelter for the oppressed.
- He is a refuge for those in trouble.

THE PROMISE
GOD EXALTS HIS SERVANTS

Whoever wants to be a leader among you must be your
servant, and whoever wants to be first must become your slave.

Matthew 20:26-27

THE world has it all backward. The world ascribes greatness to
those who are excessively ambitious. The world applauds the
proud who are willing to do almost anything to climb to the
top of the heap. To the world's way of thinking, such "drive,"
such obsession with gaining glory is the true measure of
success.

Jesus has other ideas. He tells his followers that the way up is
down. If we want to be great from heaven's perspective, we must
be willing to take the place of a lowly servant. Jesus didn't just
teach that principle, he modeled it by taking "the humble position of a slave" (Philippians 2:7).

Today as you move out into a world that has embraced
values that are diametrically opposed to the teachings of Jesus,
remember that those who are arrogant and self-serving today
will eventually face humiliation. Only the humble will be
honored in the end, when the stakes are eternal.

PRAYING GOD'S PROMISE

I live in a world, Lord, where almost everyone is fighting for the top spot, seeking power and acclaim. Give me the grace to choose the way of servanthood. I want to imitate you. Help me to put others' needs and desires before my own. Your Word teaches that true reward awaits those who humble themselves in loving service. Keep me from the tendency to be driven, to step on others, to exalt myself. Give me a servant's heart today.

GOD'S PROMISE TO YOU

● God honors those who serve.

THE PROMISE
GOD REWARDS YOUR HARD WORK

Lazy people are soon poor; hard workers get rich.

Proverbs 10:4

T H E book of Proverbs is Hebrew wisdom literature, a collection of wise sayings written in poetic form. They are essentially universal observations written by King Solomon and others with vast experience and skill in living.

As modern-day readers we are mistaken if we see these pithy maxims as absolute *promises*. Technically, they are nothing more than general *principles*—things that are normally true. Even so, we are wise to read and heed what we find in the thirty-one chapters of Proverbs.

The proverb in today's verse contrasts the lifestyles of laziness and diligence. Typically, the lazy person ends up suffering while the hard worker eventually enjoys a measure of prosperity. It's not a *guarantee*, but success is much more likely for the diligent person (see Ephesians 6:6-8).

What about you? Are you doing your best and going the extra mile? Remember: excellence almost always results in a handsome payoff!

PRAYING GOD'S PROMISE

You honor the diligent, Lord. With that in mind, I want to do my work with enthusiasm and for your glory. Keep me from a lazy spirit. Even though many around me expect something for nothing, help me to be willing to labor. Please honor my efforts in the name of Christ.

GOD'S PROMISE TO YOU

- God rewards the diligent.

THE PROMISE
GOD DIRECTS YOUR WAYS

Trust in the Lord with all your heart; do not depend on your own understanding. Seek his will in all you do, and he will direct your paths.   Proverbs 3:5-6

H ERE'S an exercise for the next time you find yourself up to your neck in question marks. Whenever you sense that the fast pace of life is pressuring you to make a quick decision and you haven't a clue which path to go down, ask yourself the following questions:

1. Am I looking to and leaning on God? Is he central in my thoughts?
2. Do I put more stock in God's counsel than in my own ideas or the opinions of others?
3. Am I open to the idea that God may very well ask me to do something that everyone else thinks is "crazy"?
4. Do I honestly want what God wants—in *every* part of my life?
5. Am I willing to wait until I have a clear sense of his leading before I act?

If you can answer yes to these questions, God promises to direct you! Is that good or what?

PRAYING GOD'S PROMISE

You want me to trust you, Lord, with all my heart. Oh God, I want to do that. You are worthy of my trust. Forgive me for the times I doubt. In times of uncertainty, I know I need more than mere human understanding. I need you! I don't want to rely just on my own thoughts or on the advice of others. I want your will. Will you show me which way to go? Remind me that seeking you often takes time and effort. In the frustrating times, remind me that good things come to those who wait on you.

GOD'S PROMISE TO YOU

● If you trust God and and seek him, he will show you the way to go.

THE PROMISE
GOD IS MOST CONCERNED WITH YOUR HEART

The Lord doesn't make decisions the way you do! People judge by outward appearance, but the Lord looks at a person's thoughts and intentions.   1 Samuel 16:7

W E live in a culture that is obsessed with youth, beauty, physical fitness, the perfect body. When does concern over one's appearance cross the line between healthy and unhealthy?

Is it wrong, for instance, to work out for hours every day? What about cosmetic surgery or spending lots of time and effort searching for the "perfect" haircut, suntan, makeup, or wardrobe?

There are no simple answers to these questions, but the promise above reminds us that God is far more interested in what's going on inside us than in how we look on the outside. It's not wrong to want to look and feel our best, but spiritual health—the condition of our hearts and minds—is much more important.

The apostle Paul's words fit well here: "Spend your time and energy in training yourself for spiritual fitness. Physical exercise has some value, but spiritual exercise is much more important, for it promises a reward in both this life and the next" (1 Timothy 4:7-8).

PRAYING GOD'S PROMISE

Lord, it's true that our world thinks external image is everything. Forgive me for the times I get overly concerned with mere appearance. That's a shallow and unbiblical way to live. You care more about the state of my heart. Grant me the wisdom and discipline to expend the necessary time and energy to care for my soul. May you be pleased more and more as you examine my thoughts and intentions.

GOD'S PROMISE TO YOU

- God doesn't evaluate you on the basis of mere externals.
- He measures you by your thoughts and intentions.

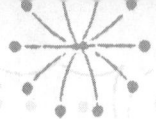

THE PROMISE
GOD IS TENDER TOWARD YOU

[The Sovereign Lord] will feed his flock like a shepherd. He will carry the lambs in his arms, holding them close to his heart. He will gently lead the mother sheep with their young.

Isaiah 40:11

S O M E of the Bible's verbal pictures of who God is inspire healthy awe and reverence: creator (Isaiah 40:28; Ephesians 3:9); ruler (2 Chronicles 20:6); lord (Exodus 3:15-18); king (Psalm 22:28; Isaiah 6:5); judge (Psalm 94:2).

Others provide a strong sense of hope, reassurance, and safety: redeemer (Isaiah 44:24); father (Psalm 103:13); friend (John 15:15; see devotion 3).

But perhaps one of the most comforting and familiar descriptions of God is that of a shepherd, the metaphor the prophet Isaiah uses in today's verse.

The overall meaning is clear. God is protective and alert. He is proactive on our behalf, always seeking our best and providing for us. But notice also these words in the verse: "in his arms," "close to his heart," "gently." Can you think of a more startling—and inviting—description of God anywhere in the Bible?

The Good Shepherd shows great tenderness to his lambs. And we are the recipients of that tenderness if we belong to him.

PRAYING GOD'S PROMISE

Shepherd of heaven, you faithfully feed and guide your flock. Thank you for your protection and provision. You are gentle with me, and you carry me in your arms and hold me close to your heart. What an amazing, jaw-dropping promise! When I am afraid or worried or tired, remind me that you look upon me and treat me with great tenderness.

GOD'S PROMISE TO YOU

- God will feed you and lead you.
- He will carry you in his arms.
- He will hold you close to his heart.

THE PROMISE
GOD HAS RESCUED YOU FROM SIN AND DEATH

God saved you by his special favor when you believed. And you can't take credit for this; it is a gift from God.

Ephesians 2:8

To say that we "can't see the forest for the trees" is to admit that, immersed in the countless details of existence, we've lost sight of the bigger picture. This phenomenon is quite common in the spiritual realm. Mired in religious busyness, we no longer ponder *"Why* did God save me?" Then, before we know it, we lose the sense of *"Wow*—did God ever save me!" Where we used to find wonder and joy, we now find only weariness and discouragement.

One solution for this common condition is to push the pause button on your hectic life and spend some time reflecting on the great salvation you have in Christ. Imagine being an enemy of God (Romans 5:10; Colossians 1:21). You once were! Consider the awful thought of your sins being counted against you. They once were! But now, because of Christ, everything is changed. You are clean, forgiven, accepted. That is God's amazing gift to you.

Don't lose sight of the "Wow!" of God's salvation.

PRAYING GOD'S PROMISE

God, you have saved me from an empty existence now and an awful existence in eternity. Thank you, Lord, for this wonderful, undeserved gift. Your love, forgiveness, life—Lord, all of these eternal blessings are a gift. Keep me from losing sight of what you've done for me. Even in the midst of a crazy, busy day, remind me of the big picture—that I am your beloved child!

GOD'S PROMISE TO YOU

- God has saved you!
- His salvation is a gift!

THE PROMISE
GOD SHOWS MERCY TO THE MERCIFUL

God blesses those who are merciful, for they will be shown
mercy.   Matthew 5:7

SOMEONE has described mercy as "not getting what we
deserve."

That's not a bad definition. The Bible says that we *deserve* to
be eternally separated from our holy God (Romans 6:23)
because of our great rebellion against him (Romans 3:23). In
other words, all we really deserve is God's judgment. But God,
in the ultimate act of mercy, offers us a full pardon and the
riches of heaven! We deserve the worst, but in Christ we get
God's very best!

Jesus talked about mercy in the Sermon on the Mount, from
which today's verse is taken. His point seems to be that if we are
truly right with God, we will extend mercy to the undeserving
people in our lives. The more mercy we show, the more of mercy
we will know. Extending mercy to someone who doesn't deserve
it is not easy. It helps to remember that we didn't deserve God's
mercy when he gave it to us in Christ.

Who are the "undeserving" in your life? Think about God's
great mercy to you, and then ask God to help you extend mercy
to those people.

PRAYING GOD'S PROMISE

God, you are merciful. Thank you for not giving me what I deserve. I deserve eternal death. Instead, I have life in Christ! Praise you, Lord God! You have said in your Word that it is the merciful who fully experience the blessings of your mercy. Forgive my pettiness. I often hold grudges and extend only conditional forgiveness. Teach me to be wild and lavish in my willingness to overlook wrongs and to bless those who don't deserve blessing.

GOD'S PROMISE TO YOU

- God blesses those who are merciful.

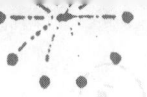
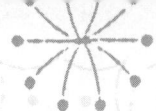
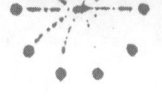

THE PROMISE
GOD GIVES YOU THE WILL TO KEEP
DOING RIGHT

God has not given us a spirit of fear and timidity, but of power, love, and self-discipline. 2 Timothy 1:7

W HEN we think of the apostle Paul, we think of the ultimate "get-it-done" person, the poster child for spiritual accomplishment. It's not hard to see why he was so effective: he was motivated, tireless, *and* fearless.

Though we marvel at such faith and courage, though we are impressed by Paul's far-flung exploits for God, most of us can't relate. In our minds Paul was a certified spiritual giant. Not us! Not now and not ever! We are much more like Timothy, Paul's young friend and protégé, who struggled with fear, feelings of inadequacy, and complacency.

In the last letter Paul ever wrote, from which today's verse is taken, he reminded Timothy that God had supplied all the resources necessary to do his will—the strength, the motivation, and the ability to stay focused on the task.

God supplies those same things to you. He will give you all that you need to enable you to do what he asks you to do. His promise is good for all his children.

PRAYING GOD'S PROMISE

I do not have to give in to the spirit of fear or timidity, Lord. I am too driven by circumstances and feelings. Forgive me for the times I walk according to what seems true to me instead of what you say is true. God, you have said in your Word that you provide power and love and self-discipline. When I turn to you, I can find the right motivation (love), the necessary strength (power), and the essential discipline I need to do your will in a way that brings you glory.

GOD'S PROMISE TO YOU

- God supplies you with power.
- He gives you love as a motivation for service.
- He provides you the resource of self-discipline.

THE PROMISE
GOD PRODUCES CHANGE IN THOSE
WHO ARE SPIRIT-FILLED

When the Holy Spirit controls our lives, he will produce this kind of fruit in us: love, joy, peace, patience, kindness, goodness, faithfulness, gentleness, and self-control.   Galatians 5:22-23

HAVE you heard about the not-so-bright raccoon that stepped into a trap? The poor thing chewed off three of its feet only to discover that it was still caught!

It is a sad truth, but a lot of people live like that raccoon. They apply the wrong solutions to their problems. They sense a need for an internal change in their lives—more joy or excitement, for instance—and they foolishly and busily resort to making external changes in an effort to find what they are looking for. Maybe they switch careers or spouses or churches or hobbies. But after they make all those external changes, they feel the same way they did before. Something is still missing inside, something all those external changes are unable to provide.

God promises us that deep, lasting change is possible only when the Holy Spirit is allowed to have his way in us. Do you want to change—deeply? Begin from the inside out. Ask the Holy Spirit to control every part of your being.

PRAYING GOD'S PROMISE

Thank you, God, for giving me your indwelling Holy Spirit. Forgive me for the times I ignore his promptings. It is only through the Spirit's power that I am changed and that I am able to live as you desire. Make me willing to obey. Give me the wisdom to see that in surrendering to you, I find the beginnings of real transformation. Produce the fruit of a pure, Christlike character in me today.

GOD'S PROMISE TO YOU

- When God's Spirit empowers you, you will be like Christ.

THE PROMISE
GOD'S SON PRAYS FOR YOU!

Jesus remains a priest forever; his priesthood will never end.
Therefore he is able, once and forever, to save everyone who
comes to God through him. He lives forever to plead with God
on their behalf.   Hebrews 7:24-25

D o you have people who pray for you regularly? If so, you probably feel blessed—and rightly so. If one or two of those praying folk
happen to be godly, mature, respected saints, that may give you
an added sense of comfort. It is a wonderful source of encourage-
ment to know that others are praying to God on your behalf.

But how much more wonderful is the news that Jesus Christ
prays for his followers continually before the throne of God! It's
true. Hebrews 7 says it. The Greek word translated "to plead with
God on their behalf" was often used in ancient times to refer to
the practice of petitioning a king on behalf of someone else.

That is what Jesus does for us: Stationed at the right hand of
God, he intercedes for us nonstop, probably in much the same
manner we find him praying for his disciples in John 17. Jesus
knows and understands our weariness, our weaknesses, our
struggles, and our fears. Who better to take those concerns to
our heavenly Father? The knowledge that Jesus prays for you
can't help but give you confidence as you live in busy, uncertain
times.

PRAYING GOD'S PROMISE

Jesus is my perfect High Priest and Savior. I praise you, Lord, for your wonderful salvation and constant care. What a comfort it is to know that Jesus prays for me continually before your throne. Thank you for the reassurance that I am covered in prayer by the ultimate "prayer warrior." I pray that my life and actions would conform to the prayers of Christ.

GOD'S PROMISE TO YOU

- God has made Jesus your great High Priest.
- Jesus is the one who saves you.
- Jesus is your representative before God's throne.

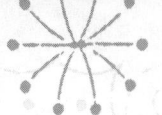

THE PROMISE
GOD CAN WORK DESPITE YOUR LIMITATIONS

Each time [I prayed, God] said, "My gracious favor is all you need. My power works best in your weakness." So now I am glad to boast about my weaknesses, so that the power of Christ may work through me.   2 Corinthians 12:9

THE Christian life is filled with apparent contradictions: We find life by losing our lives. We become leaders by living as servants. When we are weak, then we are really strong.

This last lesson is one the apostle Paul learned at a particularly difficult time in his life. Afflicted by an unnamed "thorn in the flesh," Paul begged for relief. Three times he asked God to take it away. But each time Paul asked, God said no.

In effect, the Lord told Paul, "You will have to live with this handicap. But in your extreme weakness and inability you will discover my infinite strength and ability."

What limitations or deficiencies do you see in your life? Do you focus on them as obstacles that keep you from doing your best? Or do you see them as prime opportunities to stand back and see the power of God working through your weakness? Ask God to give you Paul's perspective on those things you struggle with.

PRAYING GOD'S PROMISE

God, your grace is all I need. Teach me to see situations as you see them. Your power is displayed most clearly in my times of inability. Lord, may you receive maximum glory as I feebly lean on you and wait for you to work. I don't have to "make something happen." You will work in and through me. This is the paradox of the faith—the magnificent power of the almighty God at work in the life of a puny creature like me!

GOD'S PROMISE TO YOU

- God's grace is all you need.
- His power comes alive in your weakness.
- Hard times and weakness in your life are opportunities to trust God and to see him work through you.

THE PROMISE
GOD IS FAITHFUL TO YOU

Your faithfulness extends to every generation, as enduring as the
earth you created.   Psalm 119:90

TAKE a moment and think of some of your favorite words.
When a pollster asked respondents to list theirs, they cited such
words as *mother, home, Christmas, free,* and *vacation.*

A word that didn't make the list but should have is *faithful.*
The word *faithful* means reliable, loyal, or trustworthy. A faithful
person is one you can count on, one who will hang in there with
you until the bitter end—and beyond. Such dependability is a
rare commodity these days. Maybe that explains why *faithfulness*
and *faithful* didn't make the list.

But get this: The Bible claims—repeatedly—that God is *forever*
faithful, from one generation to another, as "enduring as the
earth."

He doesn't give up on us even when we are faithless (2 Timothy 2:13). His love and faithfulness are rock solid and unchanging. That's a promise we can take to the bank.

PRAYING GOD'S PROMISE

God, your faithfulness is eternal. Thank you for being eternally devoted to me. When I can't sense your presence or see your hand at work, help me to remember that you will never let me go. And, Lord, forgive me for my faithless heart, for the times when I don't walk close to you. Make me more loyal to you.

GOD'S PROMISE TO YOU

● God is forever faithful.

THE PROMISE
GOD IS FAIR WITH YOU

The Lord is righteous in everything he does; he is filled
with kindness.   Psalm 145:17

THE first complete sentence many young children utter is,
"That's not fair!" Kids say that a lot. And, truth be told,
grown-ups *think* it a lot. It's not hard to see why. We live in a
world filled with inequity and injustice. The people who are
most undeserving often seem to get all the breaks. Nice guys, as
the saying goes, finish last.

What's important to remember is that even though life is
unfair, God never is (Hebrews 6:10). In fact, just the opposite is
true. Because he *is* just and good (Psalm 71:16), he *loves* whatever is just and good (Psalm 33:5), and everything he *does* is just
and good (Psalm 111:7).

Now, some might quibble that Christianity itself *is* unfair.
After all, we rebel against our loving God, and his response is to
offer us forgiveness instead of condemnation?! Precisely. In a
hard-to-understand spiritual transaction, Christ takes away (and
pays for) the sins of those who believe and also gives them his
perfect righteousness (2 Corinthians 5:21). Does anyone
anywhere deserve such a sweet deal? By no means! But is it *unfair*?
Not at all. Under God's gospel plan, all sin gets punished, and all
are offered salvation. This is the mystery of grace.

The next time you are faced with an unfair situation, turn to the One who is righteous in everything he does.

PRAYING GOD'S PROMISE

I struggle, God, with living in a world where evil seems to be rewarded and good is ignored, mocked, and/or punished. Help me to keep my eyes on you and on the truth of your Word. You are righteous in all you do, Lord. You are filled with kindness. I praise you and trust you, God. One day you will make everything right. When I am being treated unfairly, help me to resist the urge to respond in kind. Instead, teach me to rely fully on your kindness and to respond in a way that reflects your righteousness in my life.

GOD'S PROMISE TO YOU

- God is always righteous.
- He is filled with kindness.

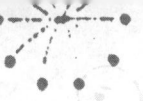
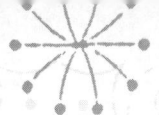
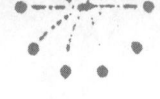

THE PROMISE
GOD SHAPES YOU THROUGH DIFFICULTY

We can rejoice, too, when we run into problems and trials,
for we know that they are good for us—they help us learn
to endure. Romans 5:3

TRUE or false: A big chunk of the busyness in our lives is
directly related to problems.

True! Imagine how much less hectic your days would be if
you and your loved ones continually enjoyed spiritual strength,
physical health, emotional stability, and financial prosperity.

Ah, but we don't live in the Garden of Eden! We live in a
thorny world filled with trials and trouble. Some days it seems
as if every time we turn around, we're dealing with a new chal-
lenge. And yet Paul says that those painful trials are actually
good for us. They make us tough and teach us to cling to God
and grow in faith and in our ability to trust him.

Today, as you're running around tending to problems in
your life, do something radical: Rejoice that you serve a God
who is so great that he turns even your biggest problems into
good (Romans 8:28; James 1:2).

PRAYING GOD'S PROMISE

Problems and trials—Lord, my life is full of them. I don't have the difficulties many have, but I do seem to stay busy trying to keep my head above water. God, you promise to use these hard times to teach me and to transform me into the person you want me to be. Help me, in faith, to learn to rejoice in difficulty, to see it as good for me. I want to better learn to endure.

GOD'S PROMISE TO YOU

- God allows you to go through trials so that you might grow and learn to endure.

THE PROMISE
GOD SHOWERS YOU WITH BLESSINGS

Praise the Lord, I tell myself, and never forget the good things he does for me. He forgives all my sins and heals all my diseases. He ransoms me from death and surrounds me with love and tender mercies. He fills my life with good things. My youth is renewed like the eagle's!   Psalm 103:2-5

MOST busy, high-energy people are list makers. They have lists for everything—letters and e-mails to write, phone calls to make, errands to run, home-improvement projects to tackle (in order of priority!), presents to buy, sites they want to see on their next vacation. The lists just go on and on.

Now, stop and think. How often do we take the time to list all the good things God has done for us? David did this in Psalm 103, and the result was spectacular. He erupted in praise as he recited the long list of amazing blessings he'd received from God.

Here's the really wonderful thing. This is not just David's list; these are also things God does for you. Which of these blessings—the "good things" listed in today's verses—do you need most today? Take some time to rejoice in God's amazing blessings to you.

PRAYING GOD'S PROMISE

You are worthy of praise, Lord, for you do countless good things for your children. Forgive me for the times I fail to acknowledge your blessings in my life. Forgiveness, healing, rescue, love, mercy—you fill my life, God, with undeserved gifts of grace. Teach me the wonderful habit of counting my blessings. I want to be a thankful person. Help me to remember today that your nature is to do for me "infinitely more than [I] would ever dare to ask or hope" (Ephesians 3:20).

GOD'S PROMISE TO YOU

- God forgives your sin.
- He heals your diseases.
- He surrounds you with love and mercy.
- He fills your life with good things.

THE PROMISE
GOD DELIVERS YOU FROM CONDEMNATION

There is no condemnation for those who belong to Christ Jesus.
Romans 8:1

ONE of the most destructive types of busyness is practiced by some professing Christians. Though outwardly they *proclaim* a gospel that promises a new, right standing with God and adoption as his beloved children, inwardly these people *practice* a very different belief.

They busy themselves with thoughts of unworthiness and guilt. They worry about whether they've displeased God in some way. They wonder whether a difficulty that arises is God's chastisement for some failing on their part. In short, they live under a self-imposed cloud of condemnation. And they do this despite the promise that followers of Jesus are free—forever!—from the threat of divine retribution.

The New Testament is clear: Christ has already taken all of the awful punishment we deserved because of our sin. No one can undo what Christ has done. So, if we are going to busy ourselves, it should be with continual praise to God for his amazing grace!

PRAYING GOD'S PROMISE

I am so grateful that you do not condemn your children, God. Forgive me for the times I wrongly think you want to punish me for my failures. Christ took my punishment, and he gave me his righteousness. Because of that you see me as perfect and precious. You do not hold my sins against me. Help me to better understand your grace and mercy so that I might be more gracious and merciful and might live in the wonderful freedom that I have in knowing that I am no longer condemned.

GOD'S PROMISE TO YOU

- As God's child you do not have to fear punishment.

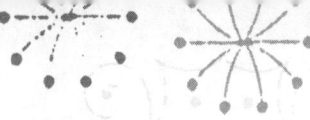

THE PROMISE
GOD HELPS YOU TO RESIST SIN

Remember that the temptations that come into your life are no different from what others experience. And God is faithful. He will keep the temptation from becoming so strong that you can't stand up against it. When you are tempted, he will show you a way out so that you will not give in to it.   1 Corinthians 10:13

GREAT *productivity* often results in great *susceptibility*—to temptation. This explains why busy, get-it-done-type people have a tendency to sin so spectacularly (e.g., extramarital affairs, financial impropriety, etc.). Too much action invariably means not enough quiet reflection. An overflowing calendar is often a sure sign of an empty soul.

The proactive solution is to make or take time daily to shore up and strengthen your spiritual life. The reactive solution in those hectic periods when sinful desires seem so powerful is to bank on the promise above. Our God is faithful to help us overcome temptation. He protects us from excessive temptation, and he *always* provides a way of escape.

Ask the Spirit of God to search you and show you potential danger spots in your life (Psalm 139:23-24). Then ask a wise Christian friend to give you an objective evaluation of your schedule for this week and your calendar for the next month.

PRAYING GOD'S PROMISE

My temptations are not unique, Lord. I am not alone in my battle with sin. Everyone struggles. Your Word says that you are faithful to protect me from irresistible temptation. Keep me from the phony excuse that "I couldn't help it!" I can help it—with your help. You promise that when I am tempted, you will show me a way out of my dilemma. Give me sensitivity to your voice so that I do not dishonor you.

GOD'S PROMISE TO YOU

- God is faithful.
- He will not allow you to be tempted more than you can stand.
- He will always provide a way of escape for you.

THE PROMISE
GOD CALMS YOUR ANXIOUS HEART

[God's] peace will guard your hearts and minds as you live in
Christ Jesus.   Philippians 4:7

Y O U can call it being mellow or laid-back or calm. Or you can
use the more biblical term: *peace.* But whatever word you
choose, imagine how wonderful it would be to live an anxiety-
free life. Imagine not getting rattled or freaked out by every trial
you encounter. Imagine your soul remaining serene even
though a storm of unexpected troubles swirls about you. Does
that possibility seem too good to be true?

According to the Bible it isn't just so much wishful thinking.
When we trade our tendency to worry for the discipline of living
"in Christ Jesus," we experience a kind of supernatural tranquil-
lity (see Isaiah 26:3) that literally protects our hearts and minds
from unsettling disquiet.

The million-dollar question then is, How do we live "in"
Christ? An ancient saint by the name of Brother Lawrence
described it simply as "practicing his presence" moment by
moment. By that he meant that we believe and remind ourselves
that Jesus is present with us—in everyday life. And then we act
like it.

PRAYING GOD'S PROMISE

Lord, in a world filled with worry, your Word speaks of peace.
Forgive my tendency to stress out. You are worthy of my trust and
confidence. Flood my heart and mind with your perfect peace.
Teach me to "live in Christ Jesus" so that worry becomes an
unwelcome stranger to my soul.

GOD'S PROMISE TO YOU

- God will give you peace when you are anxious.
- His peace is infinitely deep.
- His peace will protect your heart and mind.

THE PROMISE
GOD OFFERS YOU HIS PERFECT INSIGHT

If you need wisdom—if you want to know what God wants you to do—ask him, and he will gladly tell you. He will not resent your asking. James 1:5

"PAPER or plastic?"

"Smoking or nonsmoking?"

"Would you like fries with that?"

I think you would agree that these are no-brainer decisions, all of them. But what about those trying life situations where the choices are harder and the stakes are higher? where there doesn't seem to be a clear-cut answer at all?

You can be thankful that God has pledged to give wisdom to the humble soul who looks to him for guidance. But how do we distinguish God's counsel from the chorus of other voices in the midst of our busy lives? There are several ways. First, although the wisdom may come to us from other people, God's wisdom will *always* square with Scripture. Second, wisdom that comes from God will *always* result in bringing glory to him. And third, God's wisdom will *always* be practical and down-to-earth.

Are you facing a tough situation and find yourself in need of clarity? Ask God in faith for guidance (James 1:5-6), and then listen for the still small voice of God.

PRAYING GOD'S PROMISE

Lord, my life is so full, and I face so many hard decisions. I do need insight from above. I praise you for being the source of all wisdom. I thank you for being gentle. You are glad to help, and you do not resent my requests. Help me to remember your willingness to help in my times of trial. You promise to tell me what to do. What wonderful assurance! I do not have to navigate my way through this world alone. Help me to look to you and to wait for you to make your wisdom clear to me.

GOD'S PROMISE TO YOU

- God will give you wisdom.
- He will gladly show you what to do.
- He will never be annoyed by your request for wisdom.

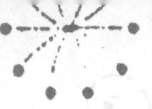
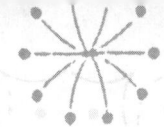

THE PROMISE
GOD HAS GIVEN YOU A NEW IDENTITY

We are citizens of heaven, where the Lord Jesus Christ lives.
And we are eagerly waiting for him to return as our Savior.

Philippians 3:20

WHAT does it mean to be "citizens of heaven"? In order to understand that phrase, we need a brief history lesson.

Philippi was a Macedonian city that became a Roman colony in 42 B.C. A few years later the Roman emperor Octavian required thousands of Italian people to relocate to Philippi. Although they were far from their homeland, these Italian expatriates enjoyed all the privileges of their full Roman citizenship.

The apostle Paul used this real-life situation to illustrate the truth that Christians are *not* natives of this earth. We're just short-term "transplants" here. Our true home (our true "country," if you will) is in heaven, and Jesus has gone to prepare a place for us there (John 14:2-3). In this world, we're "foreigners and aliens" (1 Peter 2:11), only temporary residents.

Remembering this truth can help us maintain godly priorities in a busy, hectic world.

PRAYING GOD'S PROMISE

Lord, can it really be true that my name is listed in the register of heaven? It is true! Thank you for saving me! Keep me from becoming enamored with the things of earth. Though this world screams for my attention, keep me from feeling too at home here. You are in heaven, Lord Jesus. My future is there with you. Help me to use my limited time on this earth to be an ambassador for you and for your kingdom.

GOD'S PROMISE TO YOU

- God has made you a citizen of heaven!

THE PROMISE
GOD LONGS TO BE CLOSE TO YOU

Look! Here I stand at the door and knock. If you hear me calling and open the door, I will come in, and we will share a meal as friends.   Revelation 3:20

PEOPLE often use the words of Jesus in the verse above when they are sharing the gospel with someone who doesn't know Christ. The speaker may encourage the one who is not yet a follower of Christ to "open the door of your heart and let Jesus come in, forgive you, and give you new life."

But when we look at the wider context of the verse, we see that Jesus is actually speaking to *believers,* to members of a church. Apparently these Christians had somehow gotten so busy or sidetracked that they had become indifferent to Jesus' presence in their lives!

Is this an apt description of your current situation? Is Christ, as it were, on the outside of your life (or at least on the outside of your thoughts and plans) looking in? The verse above says that he knocks. He waits. All that is required for you to once again enjoy his company is to hear him knocking and swing open the door of your soul. There he will be—your faithful, loving savior, guide, and friend.

PRAYING GOD'S PROMISE

Lord, you are always near and always desirous of my attention. Forgive me for the times I ignore you or push you to the edges of my life. You deserve the central place. Whenever I hear you calling and knocking and I open myself to you, we enjoy rich intimacy together. What a powerful promise! I know that in ancient times, sharing a meal was a sign of hospitality or deep friendship. That is what you desire, Lord—to have a close relationship with me. Please make it my desire too.

GOD'S PROMISE TO YOU

- God is near you.
- He wants your attention.
- He will be your intimate friend when you hear him knocking and open the door to him.

THE PROMISE
GOD'S TRUTH BRINGS ULTIMATE HAPPINESS

Happy are people of integrity, who follow the law of the Lord.
Happy are those who obey his decrees and search for him with
all their hearts.   Psalm 119:1-2

"DON'T worry. Be happy!" the chart-topping pop song coun-
seled. But that's not as easy as it sounds.

Here are a few observations about happiness:

1. "Being happy" is, without question, the primary goal of
   most people in our culture.
2. There is no consensus of opinion about how and where to
   find happiness. Perhaps this explains the frenetic despera-
   tion of modern life—everyone scrambling to find a kind of
   "joy of soul" that lasts more than a few hours or days.
3. The ancient Hebrew psalmist, inspired by the Spirit of
   God, stated clearly that true happiness (i.e., deep satisfaction or blessing) is bound up in understanding and obeying God's truth. In other words, those who are focused on
   the Lord and who base their lives on his unchanging Word
   are the ones who experience the wholeness of soul (integrity) that leads to rich fulfillment in life.
4. Happiness is not an end in itself. We cannot be happy
   by pursuing happiness. On the contrary, we experience

happiness as a by-product, or consequence, of seeking to know God and serve him in obedience.

PRAYING GOD'S PROMISE

I have been given your law, Lord, that I should follow it. I cannot obey what I do not know. I cannot know if I do not seek to know. Lord, stir up within me a deep hunger for your Word! You want me to seek you with all my heart. Reveal yourself and your will to me. Satisfy me with your truth. I find true, lasting happiness when I consistently live according to what is true and right. I want to be a person of integrity. Give me a greater desire to follow you and to keep your commands.

GOD'S PROMISE TO YOU

● True happiness and blessing are yours when you seek God and do what he says.

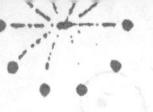
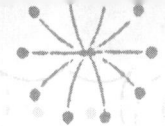
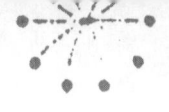

THE PROMISE
GOD IS MOLDING YOU INTO
THE IMAGE OF CHRIST

As the Spirit of the Lord works within us, we become more
and more like him and reflect his glory even more.

2 Corinthians 3:18

IN many ways change is almost imperceptible. We've all seen the
child who has grown so tall, seemingly overnight. The ivy that
has taken over the corner of the backyard. The pants that won't
fit. The savings account that is depleted.

What happened? we wonder. How and when did this change
happen?

We can see the same phenomenon in our spiritual life. God's
Spirit is at work within us all the time. Sometimes that work
takes a dramatic form, but more often it is in quiet ways that he
moves and convicts us, pushes and prods us, reveals his will to
us and empowers us. Using every possible means, God guides us
into confrontations with his truth. Why? Because his mission is
to make us just like Jesus.

Many times we may miss this subtle process of God's working in us because we're too busy focusing elsewhere. But the
promise still holds. God is making you like Jesus. Is your life
increasingly reflecting his glory?

PRAYING GOD'S PROMISE

Father, thank you for loving me enough to work in me. Make me aware of your presence. Make me cooperative with your indwelling Spirit. Your goal is to change me so that I reflect your glory. I can't always see signs of change, Lord. But I pray that others can. Mostly I pray that you can. In the words of John the Baptizer, may you increase, and may I decrease.

GOD'S PROMISE TO YOU

- God's Spirit is working in you.
- He is making you like Christ, so that you will reflect his glory.

THE PROMISE
GOD ORDERS YOUR STEPS

> The steps of the godly are directed by the Lord. He delights in every detail of their lives. Though they stumble, they will not fall, for the Lord holds them by the hand. Psalm 37:23-24

B E honest. Doesn't talk of heaven and eternity *seem* a bit unreal? Doesn't it *seem* sensible to focus on the things of this world? When we do, doesn't it *seem* as if evil has the upper hand? Don't you wonder on occasion if God really sees or cares? Sometimes, we think, he *seems* so distant, perhaps even disinterested?

David penned Psalm 37 to urge the people of God to trust their Creator and not to be shaken by the *seeming* "good life" of the godless. No matter how desperate things may appear, the truth is that God watches over his precious children. Like a doting father, he longs to walk with us, help us up when we fall, hold our hands, and steer us through trouble (Psalm 145:14; Proverbs 24:16; Micah 7:8).

No matter how you *feel* or how things *seem,* the reality is that God is there. Are you operating on the basis of what *seems* to be the case or on what God's Word says is really true? What a comfort to know that God is holding your hand!

PRAYING GOD'S PROMISE

As I walk with you, Lord, you direct my steps. Thank you for not leaving me to fend for myself. Your Word says that you delight in every detail of my life! Thank you for the assurance that you care, that you see—even when it seems you are far away. I may stumble in this life, but you promise to keep me from ultimate harm. God, I praise your name! When I feel as if I am all alone, help me to remember that things are not always what they seem. Thank you for your presence with me.

GOD'S PROMISE TO YOU

- God directs your steps.
- He delights in the details of your life.
- He will not let you fall.
- He holds your hand.

THE PROMISE
GOD RESPONDS TO YOUR CRIES

The earnest prayer of a righteous person has great power and
wonderful results.   James 5:16

PRAYER is a topic shrouded in myth. When we read reports of
ancient saints such as Martin Luther praying for two hours a
day, it's easy for us to get intimidated. Maybe someone you
respect highly has spent all night praying for a desperate situation. When you hear about that kind of prayer life, do you begin
to doubt your commitment to God and to prayer? Do the
eloquent prayers of mature, modern-day believers leave you
questioning your own faith?

Here's a memo to twenty-first-century believers: God *isn't*
monitoring our prayers with a celestial stopwatch! Neither is he
impressed by flowery phraseology!

According to the promise above, the person with the effective
prayer life is the person who simply cries out to God. "Earnest"
prayer is sincere, authentic, urgent. "Righteous" doesn't mean
perfect. "Righteous" people sin, but they quickly admit their
failures. Then, forgiven, they draw near to God again.

Are you feeling swamped? overwhelmed? hopeless? The
simple heartfelt cry, "Help!" may be the most genuine,
God-honoring prayer you've got. And it may actually be the one
that brings the best and quickest answer.

PRAYING GOD'S PROMISE

Lord, you are looking for earnest prayers from righteous hearts. Teach me to pray honestly and with authenticity, from a heart that wants, above all else, to be right with you. Show me any wrong thoughts or actions that might be hindering my communication with you. Help me to turn away from those things. According to your Word, honest, authentic, urgent prayers are powerful and effective. Thank you for listening and for responding to me when I cry out to you with integrity of heart.

GOD'S PROMISE TO YOU

- God hears the prayers of those who are right with him.
- He does big things in response to honest prayer.

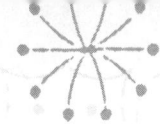

THE PROMISE
GOD TAKES CARE OF TOMORROW

Your heavenly Father already knows all your needs, and he will give you all you need from day to day if you live for him and make the Kingdom of God your primary concern. So don't worry about tomorrow, for tomorrow will bring its own worries.

Matthew 6:32-34

LISTEN to Claire. See if her words (and worries) sound familiar to you:

"I don't know what to do. My car needs work, and my daughter *really* needs braces. But we're already just barely making it, living from paycheck to paycheck. I guess I could get a second job, maybe as a salesclerk at the mall on weekends? I don't know. I just know I'm waking up—wide awake—every morning at, like, four. And I can't seem to go back to sleep."

If you're not bothered by financial worries, you're probably dealing with concerns of another kind. Maybe your child is struggling in school or your heart is breaking over a rebellious teen or your best friend just moved across the country and you don't know how you'll get along without seeing him or her every day. At times like these, remember Jesus' promise from today's verse. God sees. He knows. He cares. And best of all, he comes to the aid of those who live for him and make him their top priority.

126

Instead of panicking or fretting, instead of "preliving" a dark future that may never come, roll your burdens onto the One who cares for you (1 Peter 5:7).

PRAYING GOD'S PROMISE

God, you know every single one of my needs. I praise you for knowing all things, including every detail of my specific situation. Nothing surprises you—ever. You have promised to meet all my needs. I thank you for caring so much and for being so good. God, I experience your promise of daily provision as I live for you and make your kingdom my top concern. Help me to seek you first, to trust your gracious promise, and to keep from worrying about the future.

GOD'S PROMISE TO YOU

- God knows all your needs.
- He will meet all your daily needs as you live for him.

PART THREE

AFTERNOON PROMISES

W H Y is it that if the wheels are going to fall off, they do so in the afternoon?

We have that after-lunch lull, and then, like clockwork, moods begin to sour, responsibilities increase, and troubles multiply. Perhaps the growing tension is due to the realization that so far, our day has been less than "stellar." Or maybe we begin to stress out because we sense the coming craziness—a hundred and one things to do before quitting time or between school and mealtime or after we wolf down supper.

The following thirty promises (if we dare believe them) have the power to help us persevere. Plow through the most stressful times in your life with the help of these life-giving words of God.

THE PROMISE
GOD HAS MOVED INTO YOUR LIFE

It is God who gives us, along with you, the ability to stand firm for Christ. He has commissioned us, and he has identified us as his own by placing the Holy Spirit in our hearts as the first installment of everything he will give us.

2 Corinthians 1:21-22

C O U L D any soul living today pen a theatrical masterpiece to rival the works of William Shakespeare? Most folks don't even know what iambic pentameter is! And Shakespeare, also known as the Bard of Avon, wrote more than thirty plays and numerous poems and sonnets. It's not likely that anyone could begin to duplicate what he did. But what if "the spirit of William Shakespeare" could somehow reside in you and write through you? Suddenly the impossible *would* become possible.

The same principle is true in the Christian life. Left to our own devices we cannot really expect to accomplish very much. Can we balance our lives day in and day out? Can we live as we should? Can we exhibit godly qualities when life goes haywire? Not a chance—*unless* God lives within us.

The good news is, he does! At the moment we put our faith in Christ, God literally places his Holy Spirit inside us to give us the desire and the power to live as we should. And it is the Spirit within us who shows us that we belong to God.

Are you confused? frustrated? tired? ready to throw in the towel?

God's Spirit is in you! He will help you *if* you turn to him and ask him to.

PRAYING GOD'S PROMISE

God, you are the One who gives me the ability to stand firm for Christ. And do I ever need that ability! Most of the time I feel weak and overwhelmed and inadequate. But you have commissioned me and given me a purpose for my life. You have created me for yourself and called me to be yours. Your Holy Spirit, Lord, gives me strength and proves that I belong to you. I want to yield to you, Holy Spirit. I want to follow your lead. Let your power flow through me today, I pray.

GOD'S PROMISE TO YOU

- The ability to stand firm comes from God.
- God has commissioned you.
- He has identified you as his own by placing the Holy Spirit in your heart.

THE PROMISE
GOD HAS GIVEN YOU ALL YOU NEED

How we praise God, the Father of our Lord Jesus Christ, who has blessed us with every spiritual blessing in the heavenly realms because we belong to Christ.   Ephesians 1:3

WHEN life gets chaotic, we are prone to daydream: *If only I could stop the clock for two weeks, I could catch up. If only I could win a million bucks, my life would be simplified. If only I had _____.*

If only. If only.

In stressful times, whether our stress is self-induced or is imposed on us from external sources or circumstances over which we have no control, we are quick to look for relief through physical or material means. This is unfortunate since the things we need most in hard times are immaterial realities such as peace, patience, joy, endurance, inner strength, faithfulness, and humility.

The good news is that all of those priceless gifts are available to us right now—in limitless quantities. How do we get those gifts? By looking to God, who is the source of "every spiritual blessing." So what is the lesson for us here? Stop wishing for superficial things that don't really help, and start taking advantage of the spiritual blessings that can and will make a real difference in your life.

PRAYING GOD'S PROMISE

God, I praise you! You are the God who blesses. How easy it is to forget that you are the source of every good thing and that you yourself are good! You have blessed me with every spiritual blessing because of Christ. Your goodness to me is not because of any goodness on my part. It is all because of Christ, all because of grace. Whatever I need, Father, you have already provided. Teach me to value and utilize your infinite spiritual benefits and to seek after them more than I crave material comforts.

GOD'S PROMISE TO YOU

- Blessing comes from God.
- He has already prospered you with every spiritual blessing that you need to live in a fallen world.

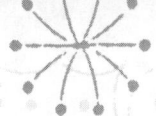
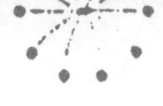

THE PROMISE
GOD COMES TO THOSE WHO WAIT

You are my strength; I wait for you to rescue me, for you,
O God, are my place of safety. In his unfailing love, my God
will come and help me.   Psalm 59:9-10

FEELING overwhelmed is an experience for some people all of
the time and for all people some of the time. The circumstances
may vary, but the end result is the same—thick dread, perhaps
even fear, a spirit of helplessness and hopelessness.

In Psalm 59 the threat facing David was the paranoid Saul
and a murderous band of assassins. Your overwhelming situation—I hope it's not hit men!—may be a calendar filled to overflowing. Just one more event to attend or the pressure of one
more responsibility to fulfill, and we feel sure we'll come
unglued.

Whatever your predicament, it's wise to follow David's example. In his time of trouble he looked up. He placed his full confidence in God's unfailing love and goodness. He believed with all
his heart that God would come through and keep him safe.

God proved himself reliable to David. He's ready to do that
for you too. When circumstances threaten to overwhelm you,
look up!

PRAYING GOD'S PROMISE

God, cause me to remember that you are my strength, my place of safety, my help. Instead of depending on my own strength or concocting a mere human solution, I need to call on you and wait on you. Your love is unfailing. Do I believe this? Do I really trust you? Oh Father, give me a heart that leans fully on you. Waiting is so hard. I am impatient. I feel weak. I want to run away. Help me to hang in there. You will rescue me. You will come and help. Give me the grace to keep trusting you to work in your way, in your time.

GOD'S PROMISE TO YOU

- God is your strength, your safety, your help.
- He will rescue you.
- His love for you never fails.

THE PROMISE
GOD SUSTAINS YOU

Praise the Lord; praise God our savior! For each day he carries us in his arms.   Psalm 68:19

"Count your blessings," urges the old hymn. "Name them one by one."

It's good counsel. Try it. Pull back from your busy life for a few minutes and ponder all that God has done for you and in you. When you do, you'll be surprised—and encouraged—by what you discover.

Psalm 68 is a record of one occasion when King David counted Israel's blessings. In that hymn David cites God's power and his fatherly compassion. By the time David gets to verse 19, he erupts in praise to the Lord.

The reason for his celebration? The promise. God "carries us in his arms." Another Bible version translates that Hebrew phrase as saying that God "daily bears our burdens" (NIV). Yet another puts it this way: "[God] daily loads us with benefits" (NKJV).

In whatever way we express it, the truth is the same: God is the One who enables us to keep going. Today (and every day) you can be confident of his concern and powerful care!

138

PRAYING GOD'S PROMISE

Lord, I praise you! You are the One who delivers. You are in control of my life and all things. Thank you, God, for going before me and with me. Thank you for saving me in numerous tough situations. You will sustain me today through whatever comes. In the same way that you watched over and accompanied the Israelites during all their journeys and victories, you are with me. When I am weighed down with care, cause me to remember that you are with me and that you care for me.

GOD'S PROMISE TO YOU

- God is the Lord.
- He is your savior.
- He carries you daily in his arms.

THE PROMISE
GOD ENCOURAGES THE DISCOURAGED

When we arrived in Macedonia there was no rest for us.
Outside there was conflict from every direction, and inside there
was fear. But God, who encourages those who are discouraged,
encouraged us by the arrival of Titus.   2 Corinthians 7:5-6

A discouraged person is one who is literally "without courage."
He or she has lost heart. Everything everywhere looks bleak.

Did you know the apostle Paul was occasionally overcome by
such a "woe is me" mind-set? Nonstop traveling, financial
shortages, ministry pressures, personal frailties, bitter opposition, concern for his converts and colleagues—add these all
together, and, yes, even the great apostle sometimes struggled
with discouragement.

But look at today's passage. At a particularly low time in his
life, the deflated apostle was encouraged by the arrival of Titus,
a longtime partner in ministry. Titus's mere presence was a
"joy" to Paul (v. 7). But this trusted friend also brought
soul-reviving greetings from the believers in Corinth: expres-
sions of love and words of concern.

That's typical of how God works when we're discouraged. He
uses fellow believers to encourage us. Could you use a shot of
courage and renewed confidence today? Ask God to send a
faithful Titus into your life.

PRAYING GOD'S PROMISE

Father, thank you for the portions of your Word that give me insight into the saints of the Bible. They were regular people just like me, in need of grace and strength and help. I often feel and face what Paul felt and faced—restlessness, external conflict, internal fear. Like Paul, I battle discouragement. I praise you, God, for being the encourager of those who are discouraged. Use any means—your Word, a memory of your past faithfulness, a Christian friend—but please, let me find a renewed sense of confidence today.

GOD'S PROMISE TO YOU

- God encourages those who are discouraged.

THE PROMISE
GOD GRANTS YOU POWER TO PERSEVERE

I can do everything with the help of Christ who gives me the
strength I need.   Philippians 4:13

A bumper sticker seen on a worn-out car that was sputtering
and smoking up a long mountain road read "I'm peddling as
fast as I can!"

Do you ever feel like that? You're giving it all you've got, but
you're still moving at what seems like a glacial pace. Those are
the stressful times when we want to pull over and quit. And yet
those are exactly the times we need the promise above.

One of the apostle Paul's continual uphill struggles was his
financial situation. Sometimes he had "plenty"; at other times
he had "almost nothing" (v. 12).

But God was always faithful to supply all that Paul needed
(v. 19). Paul learned the lesson that all of us need to learn: Even
in the most trying times, Christ is enough. He gives us the help
and strength we need to persevere. When you're ready to "pull
over and quit," look to God for the strength you need to "keep
pedaling."

PRAYING GOD'S PROMISE

I need help, Lord. I feel so weary, so tired. You have promised to give the strength I need. Without your power I don't feel I can continue. But with your help and strength, I can do whatever you ask of me. Lord, give me a second wind. I look to you in confidence and trust because I know you are faithful.

GOD'S PROMISE TO YOU

- God will help you.
- He will give you the strength you need.
- With God's strength, you will be able to do whatever is necessary.

THE PROMISE
GOD SETS YOU FREE FROM FEAR

I prayed to the Lord, and he answered me, freeing me from all my fears. Those who look to him for help will be radiant with joy.   Psalm 34:4-5

FEAR rears its head in our lives in a variety of ways. Most commonly it shows up as mild uneasiness *(What if no one shows up? What if I miss my connecting flight?)*. Occasionally this disquiet morphs into a deeper, more vexing dread *(How are we going to pay these bills? Does this mole look funny to you?)*. In rare moments we may even succumb to outright terror that completely incapacitates us. And let's not forget those poor souls who are plagued by real yet hard-to-understand phobias (e.g., phagophobia—the fear of swallowing; sciophobia—the fear of shadows) that consume their thoughts and drastically alter their way of life.

Psalm 34 indicates that the best remedy for our apprehensive and panicky moments is prayer. Mindlessly mouthing pious, well-rehearsed words isn't the answer. But when we honestly pour out our hearts to the living God, he answers. When we seek God in fearful times, we find him. In his presence fear must flee. In its place comes supernatural joy.

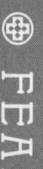

PRAYING GOD'S PROMISE

God, there are a million and one "fearful" things in this world. Too often I take my eyes off you, and I allow my mind to play the what-if game. You have promised to hear me, to answer me, to help me. Thank you for being such an attentive and good Father. I want to be free from fear and radiant with joy. Teach me to take captive my fearful thoughts and to bring them to you so that I see them from your perspective.

GOD'S PROMISE TO YOU

- God will answer your cries for help.
- He will free you from fear.
- He will give you joy.

THE PROMISE
GOD WILL USE YOU TO HELP OTHERS
KNOW HIM

Thanks be to God, who made us his captives and leads us along in Christ's triumphal procession. Now wherever we go he uses us to tell others about the Lord and to spread the Good News like a sweet perfume.   2 Corinthians 2:14

T HE urgent and unceasing demands of a busy life have a way of altering our perspective. We can feel defeated and discouraged. We can begin to lose sight of what matters most in life. In those times, it's so easy to focus only on the demands of our overloaded schedules.

The imagery in today's promise comes from ancient Roman victory processions. When a general had conquered new territory, he typically would return to the capital city of Rome with his captives in tow and with great pomp and ceremony. The smell of incense and crushed flowers would fill the air as the crowds welcomed their victorious hero.

In today's verse the apostle Paul is saying that in the ultimate victory celebration, Christ is at the head of the parade. He has conquered us with his kindness and now leads us, his "captives," in triumph. He wants to use us to fill the world with the sweet fragrance of his love.

Is that your main focus today?

PRAYING GOD'S PROMISE

You have captured my heart with your love, Lord. Thank you for changing my life by giving me life. You are the victor, Jesus, in the great spiritual conflict of the ages. You deserve all praise and honor and glory. You want me as part of your entourage to be a sweet aroma of life to all those I come in contact with. Forgive me for the times I lose the joy of my salvation, for the times I get so busy that I forget my heavenly job description. Help me to open my mouth and speak powerfully and effectively for you.

GOD'S PROMISE TO YOU

- God has captured you.
- He leads you in victory.
- He uses you to spread the good news about his Son.

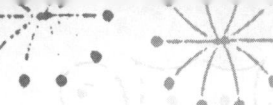

THE PROMISE
GOD WELCOMES YOU INTO HIS PRESENCE

This High Priest of ours understands our weaknesses, for he faced all of the same temptations we do, yet he did not sin. So let us come boldly to the throne of our gracious God. There we will receive his mercy, and we will find grace to help us when we need it. Hebrews 4:15-16

PROJECTION is the term psychologists use to describe our tendency to assume that others think and act the same ways we think and act—and for the same reasons. For example, we are busily trying to accomplish a long list of urgent tasks. We are focused and do not want to be bothered. But inevitably our children interrupt us or the telephone rings, and we become annoyed.

Because this is our natural reaction, we often assume that God operates the same way. We "project" our response onto God. It's a big job running the universe, we reason. And God has more important issues to address than our silly old problems. No sense bothering him. We don't want to *irritate* him.

According to today's promise, this is clearly wrong thinking—projection at its worst. God *welcomes* us into his presence. In fact, he invites us to come boldly to him. The prayers of the upright are his delight (Proverbs 15:8)!

PRAYING GOD'S PROMISE

You understand me, Lord, and my situation. I praise you for being my perfect High Priest. You know my weaknesses and understand my temptations. You invite me into your presence. You are never too busy for me! You will give me all the mercy and grace I need whenever I need them. Thank you, God, for the total, unhindered access I have to you through Christ.

GOD'S PROMISE TO YOU

- God understands your weaknesses.
- He wants you to come boldly into his presence.
- He will give you mercy and grace in your time of need.

THE PROMISE
GOD LIFTS YOU UP

You, O Lord, are a shield around me, my glory, and the one who lifts my head high.

Psalm 3:3

As you survey your life, what situation seems most hopeless to you? Is it illness? unresolved conflict? a willful child? financial struggles? (Whatever it is, you probably didn't have to think too hard to come up with your answer.)

Now consider this: When Absalom tried to steal the throne from his father, King David, the conventional wisdom was that David was history. But rather than surrender to his enemies or listen to all the naysayers, David threw himself into the strong arms of God. In his classic prayer in Psalm 3, from which today's promise comes, David first declared the apparent hopelessness of his circumstances: "I have so many enemies; so many are against me. So many are saying, 'God will never rescue him!'" (Psalm 3:1-2). Then notice what David did next: He acknowledged the Lord as the ultimate source of protection ("a shield"), honor ("my glory"), and restoration ("the one who lifts my head high").

It's not just a neat historical anecdote. It's a promise! God wants to meet us in the depths and raise us to the heights.

PRAYING GOD'S PROMISE

You are a shield about me, Lord. Keep me from faithlessly and foolishly thinking that my life or future are in jeopardy. You are my glory and the One who lifts my head. Oh God, when people or situations get me down and I'm feeling hopeless and helpless, help me to remember that you humble the proud and exalt the humble.

GOD'S PROMISE TO YOU

- God is your shield.
- He is your glory.
- He is the One who lifts your head high.

THE PROMISE
GOD BRINGS YOU THROUGH TROUBLE

[The Lord] is my loving ally and my fortress, my tower of
safety, my deliverer. He stands before me as a shield, and I
take refuge in him.   Psalm 144:2

SOME of Ireland's ancient castles contain secret rooms accessible only by tiny doorways and extremely narrow staircases. Historians note that in times of enemy attack, children were able to flee to these towers and find safety because armor-clad invaders were too big to fit through the small openings into these rooms.

Today's promise paints a great picture of the kind of protection God promises to provide for his children! He surrounds us with his love. He shields us from ultimate harm. He is our fortress and tower of safety. All that is necessary is for us to run to him and take refuge. When we do, no enemy can get to us. David experienced this reality many times, both before and after becoming king. Someone was always seeking to take his life!

If you have ever been afraid—not just mildly anxious at the thought of speaking to a group or slightly panicked at the thought of a task a bit out of your comfort zone—but *really* scared, take today's promise to heart. And say with the psalmist: "The Lord is for me, so I will not be afraid. What can mere mortals do to me?" (Psalm 118:6).

PRAYING GOD'S PROMISE

Lord, you are my loving ally. Nothing can separate me from your love. I am your child. You are my impregnable fortress, my unconquerable tower of safety. Oh God, I do believe this promise; help my unbelief! Give me an unwavering faith. You will shield me as I hide in you. I praise you for bringing me through trouble. I look to you as my sole deliverer.

GOD'S PROMISE TO YOU

- God is your loving ally.
- He is your fortress, your tower of safety.
- He will shield you when you take refuge in him.

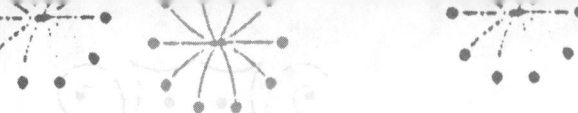

THE PROMISE
GOD USES TRIALS TO TRANSFORM YOU

Dear brothers and sisters, whenever trouble comes your way, let it be an opportunity for joy. For when your faith is tested, your endurance has a chance to grow. So let it grow, for when your endurance is fully developed, you will be strong in character and ready for anything.

James 1:2-4

TRIALS bring out the worst in people. Some turn to whining or grumbling. Others become stoic and quiet or withdrawn. Anger. Resignation. Self-pity. Manipulation. Whew! When hard times come, things can get ugly in a hurry.

According to James 1, trials can also bring out the best in people. That's God's design. He has promised to grow us up and make us like Christ (Romans 8:29)—no matter what it takes.

The interesting thing about all this is that trials are going to come—regardless of our attitude. When they do, how can you make the best of a difficult situation? Today's promise reminds you to let trials be opportunities for joy. How, you may ask, do we see an opportunity for joy in the midst of suffering? The answer is in the next sentence of the promise: Endurance grows when our faith is tested, and that results in strength of character. The process isn't always fun, but it is worthwhile. And in the midst of trouble, God will give you joy as you grow more like Christ.

PRAYING GOD'S PROMISE

You offer joy when trouble comes. Oh God, how often do I choose a bad attitude? Forgive me for being so nearsighted that I miss the big picture. Your intent is to use trials in my life to cause me to grow deeper in my faith. Keep me from fighting you, Lord. Help me to submit to your severe mercy that wants only glory for yourself and ultimate satisfaction for my soul.

GOD'S PROMISE TO YOU

- God can give you joy in troubling times.
- God uses trials to help you grow.

THE PROMISE
GOD GIVES YOU REAL POWER OVER SIN

Have you forgotten that when we became Christians and were baptized to become one with Christ Jesus, we died with him? For we died and were buried with Christ by baptism. And just as Christ was raised from the dead by the glorious power of the Father, now we also may live new lives. Since we have been united with him in his death, we will also be raised as he was.

Romans 6:3-5

A T the end of the movie *The Wizard of Oz,* after Dorothy has endured all kinds of scary adventures trying to get back to Kansas, Glenda, the good witch, casually tells Dorothy that she's *always* had the power to go home.

This is a good, if imperfect, picture of the Christian life. We put our faith in Christ and determine to follow him. But still we struggle with old sinful habits and fleshly desires. Perhaps we go off on a busy search for some kind of "magical" answer to our dilemma when all the time God has already put the real solution within us.

How is that so? Through salvation God has changed our essential nature (2 Corinthians 5:17) and linked us permanently to his Son (Colossians 3:3-4). He has also implanted his Holy Spirit within us to give us the power to live as we should.

None of this is meant to suggest that our living holy lives is as simple as Dorothy's clicking the heels of her ruby slippers together. But God does give us great and mysterious power in the promise of new life in Christ.

PRAYING GOD'S PROMISE

God, you have made me one with Christ. Somehow I was "in" him when he died, was buried, and was raised to life again. These are great mysteries and profound truths. Help me to better understand the monumental blessings and changes that salvation brings. The same power that raised Christ from the dead is available to me to live as I should. Give me eyes to see and ears to hear. Give me the faith to believe this amazing promise: As a brand-new creature, I do not have to yield to sin.

GOD'S PROMISE TO YOU

- God has joined you to Christ.
- Your old sinful nature has no power over you.
- He has given you the capacity to live a brand-new life.

THE PROMISE
GOD IS CONCERNED FOR YOU

Give all your worries and cares to God, for he cares about what happens to you.

1 Peter 5:7

WHY do we worry? It doesn't help a thing. Jesus taught that worry can't add a single moment to your life (Luke 12:25). In fact, researchers are discovering that people with high levels of anxiety are much more susceptible to long-term health problems than those who don't worry.

We seem to think that if we get worked up and stressed out over a problem, our situation will somehow improve or we will find the solution more readily. So we bite off all our nails, wring our hands, pace around, stay up nights tossing the problem around in our heads. But nothing changes, except maybe our blood pressure!

A better way of dealing with worrisome problems is to roll them over onto the shoulders of God. Only he is big enough to deal with them. And only he promises to care for us in perfect ways.

The next time you're stewing about a problem, remember today's promise—and do what it says. Give your troubles to the only One who can solve them . . . and let him soothe your worried heart.

PRAYING GOD'S PROMISE

Lord, your Word instructs me to give all my worries and cares to you. Forgive me for the foolish habit of fretting and fussing over things I can't control. You are concerned about my well-being. I don't have to burden myself trying to take care of everything by myself. You care for me, God. Teach me to trust your promise and to believe that you have my best interests at heart.

GOD'S PROMISE TO YOU

● God cares about what happens to you.

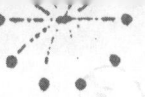
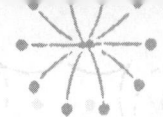
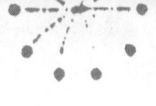

THE PROMISE
GOD HELPS YOU TO RESTRAIN YOUR
NATURAL IMPULSES

When the Holy Spirit controls our lives, he will produce this
kind of fruit in us: . . . self-control.   Galatians 5:22-23

IMAGINE a world in which people lived with complete self-
control. There would be no road rage. The word *addiction*
would disappear from our national vocabulary. Domestic-abuse
counselors would suffer from layoffs and would need to seek a
different type of employment. Children would no longer be
born out of wedlock. Our country might even experience severe
short-term economic woes as people radically reduced their
spending!

The Greek word translated "self-control" in today's promise
refers to the holding in or restraining of our passions and appe-
tites. In other words, we may *feel* like screaming at that annoy-
ing, bumbling coworker, but we don't do it. We may feel
compelled to stay at the office working for another hour or so,
but we push aside such a temptation in order to honor the
priority of family time. With the Spirit's help we do not give in
to our rampaging desires.

Self-control for the whole world is not a possibility (at least
until Christ returns). However, it *is* possible in your life today.
In what areas do you struggle with self-control? Today's prom-

ise says that when the Spirit of God controls our lives, he gives us the power to control ourselves. How are you doing in the self-control department?

PRAYING GOD'S PROMISE

Your Spirit lives in me, God. Thank you for not leaving me all alone. I praise you for the presence in my life of the Counselor, the Comforter, the One who leads me into truth and convicts me of sin. It is through the Spirit that I can manifest the fruit of self-control. Spirit of God, do not merely live in me. Control me. Change me. Fill me. I do not want to be governed by sinful impulses but by you.

GOD'S PROMISE TO YOU

- When God's Spirit reigns in your life, he will help you to have self-control.

THE PROMISE
GOD IS ABSOLUTELY RELIABLE

> Don't be afraid, for I am with you. Do not be dismayed, for I am your God. I will strengthen you. I will help you. I will uphold you with my victorious right hand.　　　　Isaiah 41:10

DISMAY is not a word that we typically use in everyday life. But it *is* a feeling we experience on a regular basis. According to *Webster's Ninth New Collegiate Dictionary* (1991), *dismay* implies that someone is "perplexed or at a loss as to how to deal with something."

Think about the stress-inducing issues you face: Conflicting vacation schedules. Continual worries about school. Daunting pressures at work. Unpleasant social obligations. New church commitments. Difficult neighbors. Any or all of these can result in dismay. You may feel as if you are "at a loss" about how to resolve these issues or to get beyond them. You may be perplexed at how to press on through situations that show no signs of being resolved anytime soon.

The good news is that God stands ready to dismiss your dismay. The process is as simple—and as difficult—as believing that he's with you, that he cares enough to do something about those situations, and that he is big enough to help you. God affirms his presence with you and promises to strengthen, help, and uphold you. Do not be dismayed!

PRAYING GOD'S PROMISE

Lord, I do not have to be afraid or dismayed—you are with me. Thank you for your presence, which drives away darkness and doubt. You offer strength and help. Lord, I desperately need those things from you. Instead of trying to solve my dilemmas myself, I want to look to you as my guide. Lift me up in the way that you see fit.

GOD'S PROMISE TO YOU

- God is with you.
- He will strengthen you.
- He will help you and lift you up.

THE PROMISE
GOD GIVES PEACE TO HIS PEOPLE

You will keep in perfect peace all who trust in you, whose thoughts are fixed on you! Trust in the Lord always, for the Lord God is the eternal Rock. Isaiah 26:3-4

TURMOIL, conflict, restlessness—these are the antonyms, or opposites, of the word *peace*. They are also accurate descriptions of the state of our own hearts much of the time.

Why do we churn with worry? What makes us so restless? More important, what is the solution to an anxious, stirred-up soul?

The Old Testament prophet Isaiah declared that perfect peace comes only to those who trust the Lord. He goes on to say that this trusting process involves fixing our thoughts on God—on who he is, what he has done, and what he is able to do. But this isn't just an Old Testament idea. We find the same type of counsel in the New Testament: "Let us run with endurance the race that God has set before us. We do this by keeping our eyes on Jesus, on whom our faith depends from start to finish. He was willing to die a shameful death on the cross because of the joy he knew would be his afterward. Now he is seated in the place of highest honor beside God's throne in heaven" (Hebrews 12:1-2).

In the midst of your busy life, where's your mind fixed?

PRAYING GOD'S PROMISE

You promise peace to those who trust in you and set their minds on you, Lord. Maybe the reason I'm so anxious so much of the time is that I take my eyes off of you. I focus on my problems. Much like Peter as he walked toward you on the water, I begin to "sink" when I stop looking at you and begin to focus on where I am. Forgive me. Help me to overcome this habit of faithlessness. Lord, you are solid and dependable. You are worthy of my full trust. I love you, Lord. You are my rock. As long as I look to you, I will not be shaken.

GOD'S PROMISE TO YOU

- God will give you perfect peace when you focus on him and trust in him.
- He is the eternal Rock.

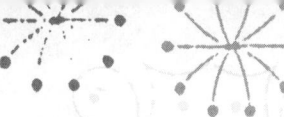

THE PROMISE
GOD NEVER CHANGES

I am the Lord, and I do not change.   Malachi 3:6

SOMETIMES we do it to ourselves: We foolishly take on too much and get in over our heads.

At other times we do things right, and we still find ourselves swept by a tidal wave of events beyond our control. Maybe we're employed one day and unemployed the next, through no fault of our own. Our finances may take a nose-dive due to some unforeseen event or need. Someone we love may suddenly turn on us and a relationship we hold dear ends without warning.

In moments of excessive stress and uncertainty, it is good to remember that we have an anchor in the storm: the constancy of God.

Theologians call this *immutability,* which is a fancy term for the fact that God is unchanging. He is not moody or unpredictable. His affection and care for us do not waver. Time does not alter God's eternal plans; neither do human choices foil his purposes.

Today's promise is concise enough to memorize. Do that, and the next time you feel overwhelmed by personal upheaval or professional chaos, find reassurance and peace in the knowledge that God never changes.

PRAYING GOD'S PROMISE

Oh Lord, you are God! Help me to remember today that I can rest in the truth that you control all things. You never change. You are the same yesterday, today, and forever! When my life is like a whirlwind and I begin to lose my bearings, give me the wisdom to anchor myself in your unchanging character.

GOD'S PROMISE TO YOU

- God is the Lord.
- He does not change.

THE PROMISE
GOD BLESSES YOU WHEN YOU TRUST HIM

Commit everything you do to the Lord. Trust him, and he will
help you.   Psalm 37:5

GOD helps those who help themselves, right?

Wrong. God helps those who *trust him*. That's the promise in
the verse above. The verb *commit* means to "roll it over on." It's a
synonym for trust.

Trusting (relying on God) requires stillness of soul and an
ongoing willingness to listen—"What is the Lord saying to me in
this situation? How and where does he want to lead me?" Trusting also requires that we *wait* (perhaps the most despised
four-letter word of this generation).

On the other hand, *trying* (helping ourselves) feeds our ego
and helps us fit in. We go to bed late and get up early because
everybody else does and because it is the productive, get-it-done
person whom our culture applauds and rewards.

Today when you feel the pressure to get busy, to make it
happen, to push ahead, to knock down doors, make sure you
first look to God and listen to him. Without his perspective,
leading, and help, you cannot find true blessing or ultimate
success.

PRAYING GOD'S PROMISE

*You have promised to help me, Lord, if I will trust you. It goes
against my old sinful nature to wait on your leading and to rely on
your strength. My tendency is to get busy in my own strength.
Forgive me, Father. Change me. Increase my faith. Help me to roll
over my endeavors onto you.*

GOD'S PROMISE TO YOU

● God helps those who trust him.

THE PROMISE
GOD PROMISES TO GROW HIS CHURCH

[Christ] is the one who gave these gifts to the church: the apostles, the prophets, the evangelists, and the pastors and teachers. Their responsibility is to equip God's people to do his work and build up the church, the body of Christ, until we come to such unity in our faith and knowledge of God's Son that we will be mature and full grown in the Lord, measuring up to the full stature of Christ. Ephesians 4:11-13

THE Thompsons are like so many other Christian families. They try to juggle a long list of *"have* to's" and just as many *"want* to's." Last weekend was typical: a soccer tournament, a recital, yard work, a dinner party, church, plus an invitation to go with friends up to the lake.

Why in situations like this do many Christians make the same choice the Thompsons made? They drop church from the weekend schedule of events. What does that say about our priorities and beliefs?

The New Testament is clear that the church—for all its many faults—is God's primary tool for growing us up in the faith. We need the church. It's only as we gather regularly with other believers in study and worship that we are challenged to grow deeper (Hebrews 10:24-25).

Our own church body also needs us. When we are lax about

regular attendance, other believers miss out on the unique gifts we have to offer.

PRAYING GOD'S PROMISE

The church is your plan, Lord, for accomplishing your will on earth. Forgive me for the times I'm critical of my church. It's not perfect, but neither am I. Help me to have a deeper appreciation for the way you have designed the body of Christ to work together. You want us to grow and mature and be one. Teach me to serve, Lord, using the gifts you've given. Remind me that if I'm too busy to play a vital role in my local church, I'm too busy.

GOD'S PROMISE TO YOU

- God gives you spiritual leaders to equip you.
- He wants to use you to help others grow, and he wants to use them to help you reach spiritual maturity.

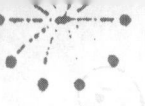
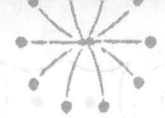

THE PROMISE
GOD HELPS YOU TO FACE YOUR FEARS

> When you go through deep waters and great trouble, I will be with you. . . . For I am the Lord, your God, the Holy One of Israel, your Savior. . . . You are precious to me . . . and I love you.
>
> Isaiah 43:2-4

L ET'S be clear. God spoke the words of Isaiah 43 for the benefit of the Jews who would one day be living in exile in Babylon. This future generation, far from their homeland and suffering discipline at the hands of God, would need comfort and courage. They would need a strong reminder in the midst of their mess that God still cared for them and had not given up on them.

As modern-day Christians we can't technically say that this particular Old Testament prophecy is a promise to us. But we can use the passage as a window into the very heart and character of God. Looking into Isaiah 43, we are reminded that God is always with us (Matthew 28:20), that he is our Savior (Titus 3:4), and that he loves us with an affection that we cannot begin to fathom (Romans 5:8; Ephesians 3:19).

Such assurances can give us the courage to face whatever troubles life brings.

PRAYING GOD'S PROMISE

You are always with me in times of great trouble. Thank you, Lord, for your constant protection and care. You are the one true God and the only One who can save. I have confidence and peace when I remember your power and might. I am precious and beloved in your sight. Can it really be, God, that you would love me? Praise you, Lord. Praise you in the highest heavens!

GOD'S PROMISE TO YOU

- God is with you in times of trouble.
- He is your God and Savior.
- You are precious to him.
- He loves you!

THE PROMISE
GOD WILL REWARD YOUR FAITHFULNESS

What we suffer now is nothing compared to the glory he will give us later.   Romans 8:18

I F this existence is all we get, why not embrace a frantic lifestyle of trying to have it all and do it all? Why not embark on an all-out quest for earthly possessions and pleasures? Such is the mind-set of many who have embraced the "busyness" lie.

On the other side are the faithful few who, by God's grace, see the temporary nature of this world. Struck by the piercing reality of the world to come, they embrace a different lifestyle. As we read in Hebrews 11:24-26, they, like Moses of old, say yes to God, which simultaneously means that they say no to most of what our culture prizes and pursues with great passion. For this they are mocked and derided. For this they suffer—sometimes greatly.

But look at today's promise from Scripture. What you may be suffering now won't last forever. What *will* last forever is the glory God will give you later. Those who persevere have a glorious future (2 Corinthians 4:16-18). God rewards the faithful, those who cling to their convictions even when the cost is great suffering.

PRAYING GOD'S PROMISE

You promise future glory to those who suffer in the present because of their faithfulness. God, give me the courage to stand with your people. Protect me from wrong and shallow ways of thinking. I don't want to suffer, but more than that, I don't want to miss your blessing or the chance to bring you honor. Remind me that walking with you is worth far more than any amount of pleasure my culture might offer me.

GOD'S PROMISE TO YOU

● God will give glory to those who suffer for doing right.

THE PROMISE
GOD LOOKS OUT FOR YOU

The Lord is kind and merciful, slow to get angry, full of
unfailing love.   Psalm 145:8

In a typical day we encounter people who are grouchy and
snippy. People who don't have a kind word for anybody. People
whose tempers have short fuses. That's just life. Get in the way
of self-centered people who are rushing about to get things
done, and you're almost certain to get run over—either physically or verbally.

The sad reality is that even Christians display such crass and
rude behavior! We occasionally succumb to the pressures of
busyness and morph into demanding and irritable people with
little patience for an elderly driver, a forgetful colleague, or a
clumsy child. Sometimes we even rationalize such behavior by
saying that we're "under a lot of pressure" or we have "too much
on our plate." But when we look at Jesus, our model of right
behavior and attitudes, we see someone who was patient and
kind, even when the crowds hounded him with incessant
requests.

Aren't you glad that God doesn't get cranky and that he
doesn't make cutting remarks about us when we err? No rolling
eyes, no looks of disgust—ever.

Only tenderness and kindness. Pure patience and love. The

next time you're close to "losing your cool," remind yourself of the example of the Savior.

PRAYING GOD'S PROMISE
Oh Lord, you are kind and full of mercy. Thank you for not treating me as I deserve. You are slow to get angry and quick to show love. I praise you, God, for never getting upset with me, for never "losing it." Help me to treat others the way you treat me and the way I want to be treated by them.

GOD'S PROMISE TO YOU
- God is kind and merciful.
- He is slow to get angry.
- He is full of unfailing love.

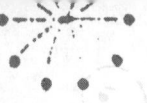
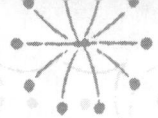

THE PROMISE
GOD BLESSES THE RIGHTEOUS

The Lord God is our light and protector. He gives us grace and glory. No good thing will the Lord withhold from those who do what is right.   Psalm 84:11

T HE words of Psalm 84 are an ancient hymn sung by Israelites who longed to go to Jerusalem and worship at the temple. What made them eager and willing to disrupt their busy lives and make such a pilgrimage?

The temple was where God made his presence known to his people and where he met with them. It was where the devout prayed, offered animal sacrifices, and found God's forgiveness and favor. In short, it was the place of grace.

Today there is no need for daily sacrifices. Christ has made the final payment for our sins. And God, instead of dwelling behind thick curtains in an ornate temple, lives within the hearts of his children.

Yet the promise above still applies. As we long for God and draw near to him (James 4:8), we experience the full riches of his grace (Ephesians 1). Because he is good, he delights in giving us good things.

PRAYING GOD'S PROMISE

You are my God, the One who provides for me and protects me.
Thank you for your glorious grace. Thank you for Christ, who died
for my sins and who makes it possible for me to experience your
presence in my life. You shower me with good things! Lord, keep me
from getting so busy that I forget to acknowledge your goodness. I
am so blessed. You have given me so much. Cause my life to reflect
your glory to those who do not yet know you.

GOD'S PROMISE TO YOU

- God is your light.
- He is your protector.
- He gives you grace and glory.
- He gives good things to those who do what is right.

THE PROMISE
GOD IS ALWAYS TRUSTWORTHY

Forever, O Lord, your word stands firm in heaven. Your faithfulness extends to every generation, as enduring as the earth
you created.   Psalm 119:89-90

A popular phrase among Christians not so long ago was "God
said it. I believe it. That settles it." Before long some believers
had modified the slogan to read: "God said it, and that settles
it—whether we believe it or not."

Their point was that God and his Word are utterly reliable. It
doesn't matter whether or not people believe what God says.
His truth is still truth, even if nobody were to believe it. What a
comfort to know that God's Word is sure—even when our faith
is shaky. And because God himself is 100 percent faithful, he is
worthy of our complete trust.

The idea here is not to clutch at a few Bible promises like a
weary and desperate mountain climber might grasp a series of
dangling ropes. We need, rather, to come to see God's Word as a
mighty mountain under our feet—strong, stable, unchanging,
and eternal. And that settles everything!

PRAYING GOD'S PROMISE

Your Word stands firm forever, Lord. I praise you for its per-manence. Heaven and earth may pass away, but your Word never will. It is reliable because you are trustworthy. You extend your enduring faithfulness to every generation. Thank you for showing your faithfulness to me day after day. I can count on you, Lord. Teach me to walk by faith. Give me the courage to stand confidently on your Word.

GOD'S PROMISE TO YOU

- God's Word is eternal and firm.
- His faithfulness to you goes on forever.

THE PROMISE
GOD SUSTAINS YOU THROUGH ROUGH TIMES

I will be your God throughout your lifetime—until your hair is white with age. I made you, and I will care for you. I will carry you along and save you.   Isaiah 46:4

PICTURE a white-haired couple celebrating their sixtieth wedding anniversary. What can we learn from them? How about selflessness and commitment, for starters? Or forgiveness and stubborn, God-honoring tenacity? Or the importance of saying, "I'm sorry. I was wrong."

Now maybe those are the obvious lessons. But there's a deeper mystery at work here too. Behind the tender devotion of these two octogenarians we catch a glimpse of the Author of love. God is the One who made them. Ask them. They'll tell you. In the rough and stormy times of life when they had nothing left, it was the Lord who sustained them and provided for them. It was the Lord who enabled them to keep their marriage vows when things took a turn "for worse," when they found themselves mired "in sickness," and when the thought of "riches" was like a cruel joke.

This is the same God who brought Israel out of foreign exile and the same God who pledges to care for you today (1 Peter 5:7) and to carry you all your days.

PRAYING GOD'S PROMISE

God, you are always with me. No matter what, I have the assurance that you are near. I cannot flee from your presence, not even if I want to. You are my maker and caretaker—the One who saves and sustains me. Oh God, use this truth in my life to give me the desire and the strength to persevere for you. I want to walk with you all the days of my life. Make me a living example of your goodness and love.

GOD'S PROMISE TO YOU

- God made you.
- He will care for you.
- He will carry you through hard times.

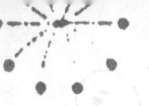
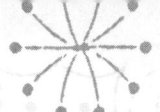

THE PROMISE
GOD USES YOUR TROUBLES FOR GOOD

We know that God causes everything to work together for the good of those who love God and are called according to his purpose for them.   Romans 8:28

HAVE you ever watched someone weave a tapestry? If we view the process from below, it looks like a disastrous mess of tangled, knotted thread. We can't even guess what the finished product will look like. A peek from above, however, reveals a work of stunning beauty. It is our perspective, of course, that makes all the difference.

That's the message of today's promise. God promises to cause everything that happens to come together in a way that benefits those who love him and are seeking to live for him. Take a moment to think about your suffering, your disappointments, your temptations, your failures—all of those tangled, knotty threads that make up your experiences and struggles. God has pledged to take all that and to transform it—somehow—into something that works out for your good.

If your life looks messy from your vantage point, just remember that God is still weaving. He knows what the finished product will look like, and the view is quite different from where he sits.

PRAYING GOD'S PROMISE

God, nothing can thwart your plans for me. I praise you for the way you orchestrate all the events of life. You are weaving a masterpiece. I trust you even though the process is painful, even though from where I sit things don't always look so pretty. You work all things together for my good. I do love you, Lord. Help me to cling to you in the darkest times of trouble.

GOD'S PROMISE TO YOU

● God causes everything to work for good in the lives of those who love and serve him.

THE PROMISE
GOD LETS YOU REAP WHAT YOU SOW

Don't be misled. Remember that you can't ignore God and get away with it. You will always reap what you sow!

Galatians 6:7

W E prefer "positive" promises, don't we? Verses that guarantee God's blessing or assure our happiness—*those* are the ones we tend to memorize and needlepoint for display on the living-room wall. So what's with the passage above? Why concentrate on such a somber portion of Scripture?

Because Galatians 6:7 *is* a promise, a troubling one to be sure, but a divine guarantee nevertheless. Here is a warning of dire consequences for those who opt for a frantic existence that excludes God and his will.

How easy it is in our culture to get swept up into thinking that a busy lifestyle is our only alternative. How natural it feels to cram our days full with activities (many of them perfectly good things), and then—*if* we happen to think of it—to try to fit God in around the edges.

God says that he must have the central place. If we ignore him and neglect what he says is important in life, we will one day find ourselves reaping a bitter harvest. And that's a *promise*.

PRAYING GOD'S PROMISE

Lord, I am prone to self-deception. Keep me from buying into my culture's attractive and popular lies. I cannot ignore you, God, without severe consequences. Give me the desire to make you supreme in my life. Make your glory my highest concern. Give me a passion for you and for the things that matter to you. You promise that ultimately I will reap whatever I sow. Lord, grant me the wisdom to live today with the future in view. Keep me from busyness. Move me to sow God-honoring thoughts and actions so that I might reap eternal rewards.

GOD'S PROMISE TO YOU

- You can't ignore God and get away with it.
- You will reap what you sow.

THE PROMISE
GOD GUARANTEES YOU A WONDERFUL FUTURE

I pray that your hearts will be flooded with light so that you can understand the wonderful future he has promised to those he called. Ephesians 1:18

MOST people express uncertainty about the future. Some worry. Some listen to a daily parade of "experts" on radio or TV. Still others read voraciously and surf the Net religiously in an attempt to spot trends. More than a few confused souls consult astrologers and other similar scam artists.

Christians should not be among these who fret about what's to come. It's true that we don't know what tomorrow holds, much less next year. In a fallen world terrible things happen. Life can turn ugly quickly, and even the righteous are not immune to times of darkness and suffering.

However, God has promised his people a wonderful future, in the ultimate sense. If you want a hint about what that wonderful future looks like, read chapters 21 and 22 of the book of Revelation. Seriously, read those chapters, and then try *not* to feel hopeful. It's hard to do.

PRAYING GOD'S PROMISE

I do need light, Lord. Help me to see, God, not just my present troubles but the future you have planned for me. Flood my heart with your light. You assure me that a wonderful future awaits. Give me an eternal perspective, Lord. Keep me from impatience and faithlessness. When troubles come, remind me that I'm not home yet and that the day is coming when you will wipe away every tear and bring an end to all mourning and pain.

GOD'S PROMISE TO YOU

- God has a wonderful future planned for you.

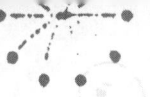
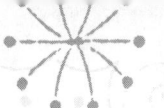
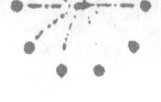

THE PROMISE
GOD HAS PREPARED AN ETERNAL HOME
FOR YOU

There are many rooms in my Father's home, and I am going to prepare a place for you. . . . When everything is ready, I will come and get you, so that you will always be with me where I am.

John 14:2-3

"THERE'S no place like home!" Dorothy admits at the sentimental climax of *The Wizard of Oz,* and we have trouble not brushing away the tears. Why do we feel such powerful yearnings for "home"?

Probably because something in us longs for a place where we are safe, secure, and comfortable. Home, ideally, is where we don't have to put on a front, where we don't need to wear "masks." It's where people love us and accept us unconditionally and welcome us with glad hearts and open arms.

It's not wrong to shop at Home Depot, read *Better Homes and Gardens,* or watch Home and Garden TV to gain ideas and knowledge about how to make your home more comfortable and attractive. But it is vital to remember that your ultimate home is in the world to come. Jesus is building a heavenly residence for you, the likes of which you cannot begin to imagine.

PRAYING GOD'S PROMISE

Lord, you are building a heavenly home for your followers. The most magnificent mansion on earth pales in comparison to the home you are building for me in heaven. I will live with you in a perfect place for all eternity. Thank you, God, for the promise that you will send Christ to get me and escort me to my true home. Help me not to get so wrapped up in the things of earth that I forget my eternal responsibilities and privileges.

GOD'S PROMISE TO YOU

- God is preparing a heavenly home for you.
- He will come for you.
- You will live with him forever.

PART FOUR

EVENING PROMISES

EVENINGS are often bittersweet.

On the one hand, we feel such sweet relief that we've managed to survive another wild-and-woolly day. On the other hand, if we're at all reflective (and you must be, or you wouldn't bother with a book like this), nighttimes are also commonly tinged with feelings of discouragement. We regret certain things we did—and sometimes things we did not do. We berate ourselves for taking on so much, and we wonder when (or if) we will ever learn to say no.

These final thirty devotions are good for those times when you feel hopeless. The verses here remind us that God is at work within us and that he never gives up on us.

THE PROMISE
GOD CHANGES YOUR MIND-SET

> This is the new covenant I will make with my people on that day, says the Lord: I will put my laws in their hearts so they will understand them, and I will write them on their minds so they will obey them.
>
> Hebrews 10:16

P E O P L E don't follow most of the laws already on the books. What makes us think they will abide by thousands of additional regulations? And yet legislators keep proposing and passing new laws all the time. We allocate more and more money each year to law enforcement. And for all our obsession with laws and rules, the evidence seems to suggest that society is getting worse.

The Bible tells us why. At the beginning of the Old Testament God made an agreement with Israel. As part of this "old covenant," God prescribed several hundred laws and commandments. Even though the people knew exactly what God expected, they lacked the capacity to obey. The mere presence of a holy code written on stone did nothing to change hearts that were inclined toward evil (Jeremiah 17:9; Romans 3:23).

At the end of the Old Testament, the prophets began speaking of a "new covenant"—not a long list of external laws but a radical, internal transformation. We experience this new covenant transformation when we trust Christ and his Spirit takes

up residence in our lives. At that moment we are funda-
mentally and forever changed. By writing his law on our
hearts, God implants within us new desires and a new way
of thinking (Romans 12:2).

PRAYING GOD'S PROMISE

*Thank you, God, for the new covenant! The old covenant showed
me your holiness and my own sin, but it did not give me the power
to change. It is the new covenant with the promise of the indwelling
Spirit that enables me to think and act differently. Guide me
according to the truth that you have written on my heart. I want to
obey you, Lord! Make me willing to do your will today.*

GOD'S PROMISE TO YOU

- God will give you a new heart and mind-set.
- He will change your desires.

THE PROMISE
GOD WILL HELP YOU TO STAND
DURING TIMES OF TROUBLE

*My help comes from the Lord, who made the heavens and the
earth! He will not let you stumble and fall; the one who
watches over you will not sleep.*   Psalm 121:2-3

W HEN busy people have problems, they often have a tendency
to look for the "quick fix." Identify the problem. Think of a
solution. Implement it. Move on. That's our preference.

We might opt to phone a trusted friend (or two or three) to
process the problem and talk about our options. Maybe we buy
and read a recommended self-help book, listen to an audiotape
series while commuting, or attend a seminar or conference
taught by a highly regarded speaker or counselor.

While none of these things are wrong (and all may actually
prove beneficial to some degree), it's important to remember
that our ultimate help comes from above. God is the One who
has the answers to our problems. He watches everything that
happens to us, and our first instinct in times of trouble should
be to turn to him and rely on him for guidance.

It's also important to realize that God may not solve our
problems quickly. In fact, he may not "solve" our problems at
all. But he does promise to help us, even if that means that he
"only" gives us the grace to keep moving forward.

PRAYING GOD'S PROMISE

Oh Lord, maker of heaven and earth, you alone provide the help I really need. Thank you for watching over me and for caring about my situation. I don't like going through troubles, but I am grateful for your constant presence. You will not allow me to suffer ultimate harm. Give me the faith, Father, to realize that no setbacks or trials are "fatal." You are bigger than any problem I face.

GOD'S PROMISE TO YOU

- God will help you.
- He will not let you stumble or fall.
- He watches over you all the time.

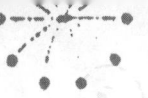
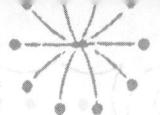
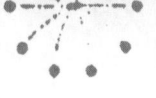

THE PROMISE
GOD GIVES PEACE IN CRAZY TIMES

I have told you all this so that you may have peace in me.
Here on earth you will have many trials and sorrows. But take
heart, because I have overcome the world.   John 16:33

FEW people in this world have ever known true peace. Most live in a chronic state of trepidation. In uneventful times they find plenty about which to be anxious. And when life gets *really* nerve-racking, they practically come unglued.

You might think that it's just irreligious people who fit this description. But, sad to say, God's people are often some of the most anxious and worrisome folks around.

But look at the promise of Christ, the One the prophets called the "Prince of Peace" (Isaiah 9:6). He offers his followers peace . . . *in him*. Christ readily admits that life in this world is characterized by "many trials and sorrows." But the reason he can assure us of his peace is that he has "overcome the world."

If we know that Christ has already "won," maybe we lack peace because we're not living in his will and trusting in his Word.

In the darkest times and saddest moments this world can throw at you, take heart. Jesus has overcome the world, and that knowledge is a source of true peace.

PRAYING GOD'S PROMISE

You want your followers to have peace in you, Lord. Forgive my habits of worry. Help me to learn to rest in you, to draw near to you in good times and bad. I know I will have troubles in this world. Remind me that you have overcome the world. Thank you, Jesus, for the promise of victory in you. In tough times teach me to look to you and lean on you. Make me an example of your supernatural peace.

GOD'S PROMISE TO YOU

- You will have troubles in this life.
- During worldly trials and sorrows, you can find peace in God.
- Jesus has overcome the world.

THE PROMISE
GOD WILL HUMBLE THE PROUD
AND EXALT THE HUMBLE

The Scriptures say, "God sets himself against the proud, but he shows favor to the humble."   James 4:6

WHAT important person do you know whose phone doesn't ring off the wall? What powerful individual have you ever heard of who has an empty appointment book or a blank calendar page?

No, the fact of the matter is that almost all prominent people lead hectic lives. They are sought out, consulted, included, and invited—all the things that most of us aspire to be.

But if we are not careful, our desires to achieve and acquire, to do more and have more than others—in short, to be successful and in demand—can seduce us into embracing a lifestyle of busyness. The root of such choices is nothing more than human pride, a quality that provokes God's displeasure. Far better to seek out a quiet life that goes against the cultural flow. But be careful here too. If we're not vigilant, we can become spiritually proud of our good decision to forsake an overly busy life!

PRAYING GOD'S PROMISE

Lord, you oppose the proud. Keep me from exalting myself, from being full of myself, from thinking myself better than or more important than others. It is not the busy person who is special, but the person who walks in your will. You show favor to the humble. Help me not to worry about keeping up with (or surpassing) the proverbial Joneses. Teach me instead the inherent blessing in a lifestyle that moves at your pace rather than at the world's.

GOD'S PROMISE TO YOU

- God opposes the proud.
- He shows favor to the humble.

THE PROMISE
GOD UNDERSTANDS YOUR TEMPTATIONS

We have a great High Priest who has gone to heaven, Jesus the Son of God. Let us cling to him and never stop trusting him. This High Priest of ours understands our weaknesses, for he faced all of the same temptations we do, yet he did not sin.

Hebrews 4:14-15

HAVE you ever been in this place? You've taken on too many responsibilities, and now you're scrambling to get it all done. People are not cooperating. Your stress level is rising even as your mood is deteriorating. Success looks doubtful.

To make matters worse, because of your busyness you haven't taken time out to make sure that you're approaching the situation from God's perspective and with his wisdom. Just when the external pressure is greatest, your inner strength is waning. There's a lesson here: *Busy people have a common tendency to lower their spiritual guard.* In their busyness they may not even realize that they're in a precarious position that leaves them open to temptation.

The good news is that when we find ourselves in places of temptation, no matter what the source, we have One to whom we can turn. He understands our weaknesses and promises to help us if we cling to him.

PRAYING GOD'S PROMISE

Jesus, you are the perfect High Priest. Thank you for understanding my unique situation and for representing me perfectly before a holy God. Apart from you, I would have no hope. I praise you because you understand me through and through—you know my weaknesses, my needs, and the way to victory. I want to cling to you and trust you. I want to face this situation without yielding to temptation.

GOD'S PROMISE TO YOU

- You have a heavenly High Priest.
- Jesus understands your weaknesses.

THE PROMISE
GOD CAN MAKE YOU CONTENT WITH LESS

True religion with contentment is great wealth. After all, we didn't bring anything with us when we came into the world, and we certainly cannot carry anything with us when we die. So if we have enough food and clothing, let us be content.

1 Timothy 6:6-8

OFTEN, the thing that drives busyness is discontent. Something vital is missing, we imagine. And if we can just find that "something," whatever it is, and make it our own, whatever it takes, we'll be happy and satisfied.

Contentment, on the other hand, is the opposite, laid-back state of mind that smiles and says, "I have everything I really need. Things are good. I'm satisfied. I will relax and enjoy my lot in life." Contented people don't typically become workaholics or overfill their appointment books or get themselves deeply into debt. For the contented, less is more—or at least it's enough.

Today's promise reminds us that ultimate contentment isn't found in the stuff of this world. Material possessions don't last, and we can't take them with us when we die. (Have you ever seen a hearse pulling a U-Haul trailer?)

When we get right down to it, if we know God and have our basic needs met, what do we have to complain about?

PRAYING GOD'S PROMISE

Contentment is your goal for me, Lord. Forgive me for the times I get discontented. Make me happy with less. Teach me to focus on all I do have rather than on the things I lack. I cannot take material possessions with me to heaven. With that in mind, Lord, give me the wisdom to focus on what lasts—your Word and the souls of those around me. Help me to make relationships—with you and others—my top priority.

GOD'S PROMISE TO YOU

- True wealth is being contented with knowing God.
- You can't take your riches into the life to come.
- God can make you content with the basics of life.

THE PROMISE
GOD LIBERATES YOU FROM TROUBLE

I cried out to the Lord in my suffering, and he heard me. He
set me free from all my fears.   Psalm 34:6

H A V E you ever felt that the Lord is turning a deaf ear to your
cries? It sometimes feels that way, doesn't it? We cry out our
needs or desires, but our desperate prayers seem to bounce
weakly off the ceiling. We may feel as if no one is listening or
even as if God isn't really there. But don't be fooled. He hears.

We sometimes imagine that God has chosen not to help us
when we are in trouble. Maybe he's angry with us, we think, or
busy solving more serious problems elsewhere in the world. But
don't kid yourself. He *is* at work in your situation—and in you.

No matter what we think or how we feel, God is a compassionate Father. Our feelings don't change that. He may not
solve our problems in the way we'd like. He doesn't always work
according to our timetable, but the promise above assures us
that God does listen to those who cry out to him. Those who
turn to him *will* find help—and courage—in times of adversity.

PRAYING GOD'S PROMISE

Lord, you hear my cries when I'm in trouble. What a blessing to know you care for me! Thank you for being a loving God! Thank you for listening to my pleas. You will set me free from all my fears. Teach me to cast my cares on you . . . and leave them there. I want to live in actual confidence and not be enslaved to potential terrors.

GOD'S PROMISE TO YOU

- God hears your cries when you are in trouble.
- He will set you free from your fears.

THE PROMISE
GOD GIVES SUCCESS IN FIGHTING
AGAINST SATAN

Humble yourselves before God. Resist the Devil, and he will flee
from you.   James 4:7

SOMEONE has quipped that temptations are like stray cats—if
you treat one nicely, it'll be back shortly with a whole bunch of
its friends! There's a lot of truth in that old joke. The more we
yield to sin and temptation, the more enticements to sin we
seem to encounter.

But the opposite is also true. The more firmly and consistently we resist the temptations that Satan puts in our path, the
stronger our resolve becomes. Sin becomes less attractive. And
Christlike holiness becomes more desirable.

It's worth noting that when Jesus bluntly rejected Satan's
overtures in the wilderness (Luke 4:1-13), the devil departed. He
didn't leave for good, and he didn't give up his diabolical fight
to undermine Jesus and his earthly ministry. But Satan did get
a small taste of his ultimate defeat and humiliation, which is
the same thing he gets whenever we tell him to take a hike
(Romans 16:20).

PRAYING GOD'S PROMISE

I want to humble myself before you, God. I am weak. I cannot live as I should without your help and power. Your Word says that if I resist the devil, he will flee. Oh God, my enemy is strong and sinister. But you are stronger. Give me the grace to recognize the attacks of the enemy and the strength to spurn his sinful offers.

GOD'S PROMISE TO YOU

- If you firmly resist Satan, he will flee from you.

THE PROMISE
GOD WILL PURIFY YOU

May the God of peace make you holy in every way, and may your whole spirit and soul and body be kept blameless until that day when our Lord Jesus Christ comes again.

1 Thessalonians 5:23

S O M E years ago Charles Swindoll wrote a book about the Christian life entitled *Three Steps Forward, Two Steps Back*.

If you've been a follower of Christ for any length of time, you know that that book title is an apt description of the journey of faith. Our experience is full of stops and starts, hits and misses, ups and downs. We think we're making progress one day only to encounter some kind of unexpected obstacle the next. When the smoke clears after a day of spiritual setbacks, we feel even further from our goal. On a day like that, we may wonder whether we're making any progess at all.

But in the midst of our struggle comes the promise that God *is* making us holy. He is transforming us from within, bringing the new life of the soul to the surface of our lives. He is fully committed to the process of purification within us. And he will guard us and keep us from falling until the day of Christ's return.

PRAYING GOD'S PROMISE

God of peace, do your work of holiness within me. I want to honor you with my life. I want to resist sin today. But at the same time, I confess that something within me often finds evil attractive. Keep me blameless. Give me a love for you and a zeal for your glory that far surpasses any impure passion. You are coming back, Lord Jesus. Help me live today in eager expectation of that blessed event. May today be a day of great spiritual progress in my life.

GOD'S PROMISE TO YOU

- God will make you holy.
- He will keep you holy.

THE PROMISE
GOD NEVER STOPS LOVING YOU

Nothing can ever separate us from his love. Death can't, and life can't. The angels can't, and the demons can't. Our fears for today, our worries about tomorrow, and even the powers of hell can't keep God's love away.   Romans 8:38

M O S T of what our world calls love is conditional affection. You get to be on the receiving end only if or because you are a certain way or you do certain things. Just stop being "that way" or doing "those things" and watch how quickly the "love" someone professes to have for you disappears.

Now ponder the love of God. His love is unconditional, permanent, sure. Like sunlight, it shines on us no matter what we do or don't do. We can't cause it to burn more brightly. We can't possibly cause it to dim. It is the great constant in life—the one thing we can't evade or do anything to change.

Certain sins in our lives might prevent us from experiencing a deep sense of God's love for a time, but sin does not diminish God's love for us any more than a few clouds diminish the sun. When we belong to God, nothing inside us or outside us can make God stop loving us with perfect, unconditional love.

Take time today to bask in the warmth of his love for you.

PRAYING GOD'S PROMISE

Your love is permanent, Lord. Transform me as I understand more deeply your undying affection for me. When I am in situations where I cannot sense your love, give me the faith to trust that you are still there and that I am always in your care.

GOD'S PROMISE TO YOU

- Nothing can separate you from God's love.

THE PROMISE
GOD MAKES YOU ABLE

We are confident of all this because of our great trust in God
through Christ. It is not that we think we can do anything of
lasting value by ourselves. Our only power and success come
from God.   2 Corinthians 3:4-5

In what situations do you feel incompetent or ineffective?
Maybe you lack a certain personality trait. Perhaps you're inex-
perienced or untrained for a certain task you need to accomplish.

The apostle Paul was familiar with such feelings. Once, he
was concerned about the young church he had begun in
Corinth. The believers there were struggling—not always
successfully—to live for God in a godless culture. To make
matters worse, a band of false teachers had come along and had
begun to question Paul's motives and to attempt to undermine
all his ministry efforts.

In the face of such pressure and opposition, Paul might have
limped away into the darkness. Instead, he remembered that
God gives strength in weakness (2 Corinthians 12:9-10). He
plowed ahead, relying fully on God and believing that God
would somehow work in and through him in spite of his own
limitations. And, of course, God did.

There are lessons galore for us here. But the biggest is this

simple truth: God is able to make you able. Commit your work to the Lord, do your best, and leave the outcome to God.

PRAYING GOD'S PROMISE

Lord, true confidence comes when I trust in you. Teach me the art of looking at you instead of at my problems and limitations. Remind me that anything of lasting value in my life is because of you, not me. Power and success come from you, God. Give me eyes of faith, that I might press on, even when I feel I'm in over my head. For when I'm weak, then you are strong.

GOD'S PROMISE TO YOU

- God is the source of your power and success.
- He gives you the ability to make a lasting impact.

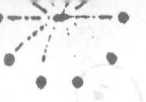
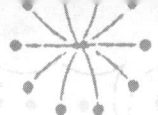

THE PROMISE
GOD WANTS TO DO MORE THAN
YOU CAN IMAGINE

Now glory be to God! By his mighty power at work within us, he is able to accomplish infinitely more than we would ever dare to ask or hope.   Ephesians 3:20

T H E record of God's people is a record of the unthinkable and the unimaginable: A ninety-year-old woman named Sarah makes her first trip to the maternity ward. A nation of slaves conquers the greatest empire in the world. A small shepherd boy goes one-on-one with the fiercest warrior of his time—and wins, eventually becoming the Israelites' most beloved king.

Both the Bible and history confirm that such hard-to-believe events are commonplace when people of faith dare to believe that God will do all he says he will do.

Take a few moments to do a little sanctified daydreaming. Given your unique background, abilities, experiences, and desires, what do you suppose God could do in your life and through your life if you were completely committed to his plan and purpose for you? God's Word says that he is able to do "infinitely more than we would ever dare to ask or hope."

Considering today's promise, whatever lofty visions you're seeing in your daydreams are probably not grand enough.

PRAYING GOD'S PROMISE

God, I praise you! You are magnificent, glorious, and awesome. You possess all power and wisdom. Forgive me for having such a small view of you and your will. You are able to do amazing things in and through me. Lord, increase my faith. Give me a bigger vision for what my life can be when you work in and through me. Grant that I might know your will for me and that I might have the courage to pursue it with passion and excitement.

GOD'S PROMISE TO YOU

- God is at work in you with his limitless power.
- He wants to do more in and through you than you can even imagine.

THE PROMISE
GOD PROMISES YOU PEACE

Don't worry about anything; instead, pray about everything. Tell God what you need, and thank him for all he has done. If you do this, you will experience God's peace, which is far more wonderful than the human mind can understand.

Philippians 4:6-7

WHAT'S the solution for someone whose stomach is in knots? Prilosec? Valium? A vacation at the beach? A weekend getaway full of amusement and fun?

Such common remedies might offer temporary relief from stress, but the long-term, ongoing answer for anxiety is prayer. Pouring out your heart to God. Honestly sharing your needs with him. Thinking about all that he has done for you and thanking him for those things.

When we pray, it's not as if we're telling God things he doesn't know. And we're not guaranteed everything we ask for. But we can be sure that when we pray, we will always get at least two things: God's listening ear and God's heart. And if we linger in his presence long enough to get his perspective, we will also find his perfect peace (Isaiah 26:3).

Prayer isn't magic. But when we talk to God honestly and in simple faith, it's pretty close.

PRAYING GOD'S PROMISE

God, keep me praying instead of worrying. Teach me the art of thankfulness. You promise peace—wonderful, supernatural peace—to those who look to you. Lord, in an anxious world, what a blessed promise—the promise of peace! I want to know that peace. And I can, by knowing you.

GOD'S PROMISE TO YOU

- If you pray about your concerns, God will give you his peace.
- God's peace is too wonderful for you to comprehend.
- His peace will guard your heart and mind.

THE PROMISE
GOD PLEDGES TO TRAIN YOU

The Lord disciplines those he loves, and he punishes those he accepts as his children.   Hebrews 12:6

DOES God "punish" us?

If we define *punishment* as making us pay for the wrongs we've committed, then the answer is a resounding no!

The Bible records in Genesis 3 how our ancestors, Adam and Eve, inexplicably rebelled against God. Divine justice called for a death sentence for all sinful humanity. Jesus, however, endured the very punishment we deserved. On the cross, he took our place, paying for our sins with his own life. Now, with our sin paid for, reconciliation with God is possible. When we trust in Christ, we receive a full pardon and become children of God (John 1:12).

As members of God's forever family, we don't have to fear his punishment, but we *are* subject to our heavenly Father's "discipline." Discipline is the corrective action a parent uses to train a child in the right way to go. Discipline is never pleasant—one possible translation of the Greek word for "punishes," above, is "whips"!—but discipline *is* a vivid reminder of God's love. He cares too much to let his children move in destructive directions.

PRAYING GOD'S PROMISE

Lord, your discipline is a sign of your love for me. Help me, God, to have the wisdom to turn away from evil before I have to face stern corrective measures. I don't want to dishonor you or suffer needlessly. Thank you for being a loving Father. It is good to know that your love is tough enough to hold me to a standard.

GOD'S PROMISE TO YOU

- God disciplines you because you are his child and he loves you.

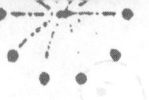
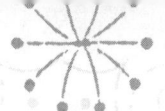
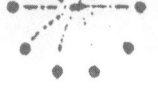

THE PROMISE
GOD BLESSES THOSE WHO CLING TO HIM

Blessed are those who trust in the Lord and have made the Lord their hope and confidence. They are like trees planted along a riverbank, with roots that reach deep into the water. Such trees are not bothered by the heat or worried by long months of drought. Their leaves stay green, and they go right on producing delicious fruit. *Jeremiah 17:7-8*

SHEEP and goats. Wheat and tares. The wise man and the foolish man. The blessed and the cursed.

Did you ever notice how the Bible repeatedly divides people into two categories? One bunch consistently looks to God in faith and seeks to serve him. The other group largely ignores God and lives independently of him.

God moved the prophet Jeremiah to picture those who rely on God and obey his Word as being vibrant and fruitful, like lush trees blossoming alongside a river. Then Jeremiah compared those who shut God out of their lives to dry shrubs in a barren desert: They have no real life and produce no fruit.

It's a vivid contrast. And it's an image that should reinforce our desire to be people who are not so busy that we shut God out of our lives.

PRAYING GOD'S PROMISE

You are my hope and confidence, Lord. I trust in you. Draw me ever closer to you, and give me a passion to seek you. I want to be fruitful even during life's hard times. It is only when I put my roots deep into you and your Word that I am able to endure dry spiritual times. Grant me a stronger and more tenacious faith.

GOD'S PROMISE TO YOU

- God blesses those who trust him.
- When you trust God, you will prosper and bear fruit even in hard times.

THE PROMISE
GOD ASSURES YOU OF TRIUMPH
IF YOU DON'T GIVE UP

Don't get tired of doing what is good. Don't get discouraged and give up, for we will reap a harvest of blessing at the appropriate time.
Galatians 6:9

L EE is a stay-at-home mom who fills her life caring for a husband, two active children, assorted friends and neighbors, a pet or two, a rose garden, and a little brick bungalow. Her days begin early and end late.

Many nights when her weary head hits the pillow, Lee doesn't have much to show for all her labors. The house doesn't stay clean very long. The laundry hamper is always overflowing. She no sooner cleans up the kitchen from one meal than she needs to start thinking about the next. The needs of her loved ones seem endless.

Are all my efforts worth it? she wonders in the darkness. *Why do I feel as if I'm only spinning my wheels?*

Lee needs the reassurance that today's promise gives: There *is* a payoff for long-term faithfulness. Keep doing right. Press on even when you feel discouraged.

God sees our efforts. And one day he will reward us for our diligent labors.

226

PRAYING GOD'S PROMISE

Sometimes, Lord, I want to give up! Remind me that you see. You do reward faithfulness. I want to do right. I want to please you. Help me to keep on keeping on. I will reap a harvest of blessing if I persevere. May the knowledge of your goodness keep me going when I feel like quitting.

GOD'S PROMISE TO YOU

- If you keep doing good, you will reap a harvest of blessing.

THE PROMISE
GOD IS LONG-SUFFERING

God had mercy on me, so that Christ Jesus could use me as a prime example of his great patience with even the worst sinners. Then others will realize that they, too, can believe in him and receive eternal life.   1 Timothy 1:16

W HO do you think is the most evil person ever to have lived? Hitler? Caligula? Jack the Ripper? Charles Manson? Attila the Hun? Or the apostle Paul?

Yes, you read that right. In inspired Scripture, Paul of Tarsus claimed to be the worst of all sinners (1 Timothy 1:15).

Apparently Paul viewed himself in this way because of his preconversion participation in arresting and killing the followers of Jesus. Paul didn't commit a onetime crime of passion either. Rather, Paul undertook a cold, calculated campaign of persecution built on fierce religious hatred for early believers.

The memories of his old life always seemed to fill Paul with deep regret. But they also filled him with wonder at the infinite patience and grace of God.

No sins are so great that God cannot forgive them. No sinner who humbles himself before God will ever be turned away. God longs to bless, not judge (2 Peter 3:9).

PRAYING GOD'S PROMISE

You show mercy, Lord. Thank you for not treating me as my sins deserve. You are patient toward sinners. Help me to use my testimony to encourage others to seek your mercy and grace. What you have done in my life, you will also do for others.

GOD'S PROMISE TO YOU

- God is patient and merciful.
- He forgives sinners and gives them eternal life when they come to him.

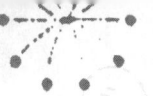
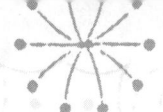

THE PROMISE
GOD SPARES THE FAITHFUL FROM DISGRACE

To you, O Lord, I lift up my soul. I trust in you, my God! Do not let me be disgraced, or let my enemies rejoice in my defeat. No one who trusts in you will ever be disgraced, but disgrace comes to those who try to deceive others. Psalm 25:1-3

A dying father once told his teenage son, "Make sure you are right with God, and you will have nothing to fear."

Those are wise words.

Others may question our actions, mock us, or even spread vicious rumors about us, but if we know in our heart of hearts that we are walking with God and honoring him, we never have to fret over the evil intents of others. As beloved children of God we can never be "disgraced" because that word literally means to be without grace. Such a description is never true of a follower of Jesus! When we belong to him, we are always in his care. We are always loved and favored and accepted as his very own.

Trust the Lord. Serve him. Then, no matter what happens, you'll be able to hold your head high, knowing that you can never be truly "disgraced" and that God will vindicate you in the end.

PRAYING GOD'S PROMISE

I lift my soul to you, Lord. You are God . . . and you are good. I trust you. No one who walks with you can ever be shamed. As long as I know that I am pleasing you, it doesn't matter what others say or do to me. I believe that you will make all things right in the end.

GOD'S PROMISE TO YOU

● God will not allow his faithful ones to be disgraced.

THE PROMISE
GOD PROVIDES SUPERNATURAL STRENGTH

God is working in you, giving you the desire to obey him and the power to do what pleases him.   Philippians 2:13

G O D wants us to live by *faith* (2 Corinthians 5:7; Hebrews 11:1). Many times, however, we live by fickle, superficial *feelings*. If we aren't especially *moved* to pray or read the Bible or reach out to a neighbor, we normally do not. If we don't *sense* God's strength surging through us, we usually confess weakness and choose to do nothing. The result of this feelings-based approach to the spiritual life is often an unsatisfying, up-and-down Christian experience.

Now, consider the promise above. It says that God is at work within us, giving us the *desire* to do right. This means we can never honestly say, "I don't *feel* like obeying." According to today's verse, God causes us to want to please him. And the promise is not only for new *desires*. It also guarantees the necessary *power* to do what God wants us to do.

In light of these truths, the question is, Why would any Christian choose to keep riding the "feelings roller coaster" when God offers a radical new way to live?

PRAYING GOD'S PROMISE

God, you are at work within me. Teach me to obey even when I feel no desire to do what is right (especially then!). You give me new desires and new power to live as I should. Bring to the surface the deep longings that you have already put inside me. Wean me from the inadequate and immature excuse that "I'm too weak." Your strength is sufficient for whatever I'm facing.

GOD'S PROMISE TO YOU

- God is at work in you.
- He gives you the desire to obey him.
- He supplies you with the power to do what pleases him.

THE PROMISE
GOD KNOWS YOU INTIMATELY

O Lord, you have examined my heart and know everything about me. You know when I sit down or stand up. You know my every thought when far away. Psalm 139:1-2

CHANCES are pretty good that as you rush through a typically hectic week, you sometimes feel that others don't understand you. Maybe a coworker gives you a strange look or a family member overreacts to an innocent remark you made.

Chances are also good that on some days you don't even understand yourself. "Why did I act that way?" you sigh. Or you wonder, *What in the world made me say that?*

Well, here's a bit of comfort from today's promise: God understands you completely. He made you, and he knows exactly what makes you tick. Your thoughts, your whereabouts, your needs—God sees them all.

So the next time you or others are having trouble getting a handle on *you*, turn to the One who knows everything about you and has perfect insight into your heart. Take comfort and peace from the reality of his absolute love and acceptance.

PRAYING GOD'S PROMISE

You have examined my heart, God, and you see me as I truly am—my failings and flaws as well as my successes. Thank you for accepting me and for choosing to love and care for me. You know everything about me—my comings and goings, even my thoughts. Help me, Father, to find comfort and rest in your love.

GOD'S PROMISE TO YOU

- God sees your heart.
- He knows your thoughts, your actions—everything about you.

THE PROMISE
GOD IS YOUR SOURCE

Riches and honor come from you alone, for you rule over everything. Power and might are in your hand, and it is at your
discretion that people are made great and given strength.

1 Chronicles 29:12

HAVE you ever experienced those occasions in life when all of
your busy labors pay off? Maybe the business deal or special
event comes together perfectly. A boss notices your hard work,
and you get a promotion, a bonus, or a raise. Maybe you spend
the day cleaning the house and cooking a wonderful dinner,
and your children chatter happily through the meal—no argu-
ments! no spills!—and actually thank you for the great meal
when they're through eating. These are wonderful
moments—wonderful and dangerous. To what or whom will we
attribute our success?

At the end of King David's reign he commissioned a national
offering for the soon-to-be-built temple. The people's response
was overwhelming. Looking at their lavish gifts of silver, gold,
and precious gems, David stood before the people and praised
. . . God! The great Hebrew king recognized the same truth we
read in the New Testament: "Whatever is good and perfect
comes to us from God above" (James 1:17).

PRAYING GOD'S PROMISE

God, you are in control of all things. Help me to remember that you rule the universe and my life. You are the source of all good things—wealth, power, and honor. What do I have, Lord, that I did not receive from you? You gave me health, intelligence, education, and opportunity. You blessed me with skill. Any success that I have and all that I am I owe to you.

GOD'S PROMISE TO YOU

- God rules over everything.
- He is the source of all riches and honor.
- He possesses all power and might.
- He is the One who gives strength and makes great.

THE PROMISE
GOD OFFERS TO TAKE YOUR HEAVY LOAD

Jesus said, "Come to me, all of you who are weary and carry heavy burdens, and I will give you rest. Take my yoke upon you. Let me teach you, because I am humble and gentle, and you will find rest for your souls. For my yoke fits perfectly, and the burden I give you is light." Matthew 11:28-30

OFTEN, the way to fix physical weariness is simply to enjoy a good meal and a good night's sleep or in extreme cases, a solid week of R and R. That's usually enough to refresh us and get us ready to get back into action. Emotional and spiritual weariness, on the other hand, are different issues altogether.

What do we do when our souls feel weighed down with care or guilt or shame? The world sure isn't very sympathetic. Oh, it may offer temporary escapes, short-term pleasures to medicate our pain. But can it offer a *cure* for the disease of spiritual heaviness? No.

Well, then, where do we turn? The truth is, such a cure is available only in Christ. He beckons the hurting and heavy-hearted to come to him. And he promises that when we do, he will deal gently with us, share and lighten our load, and give us rest.

In a frantic, stressful world, is there a better promise to be found anywhere?

PRAYING GOD'S PROMISE

Lord, you call to those who are weary and burdened, to those in desperate need of rest. Though I know you, I need to know more of you. I long to experience true rest. I trust you, Lord, because you are humble and gentle. Why would I ever look anywhere else? No one cares for me the way you do. I want to swap my heavy burden for the lighter load that you offer. Revive me. Renew me. Restore me. I want to serve you, doing your will with the strength that only you can provide.

GOD'S PROMISE TO YOU

- Jesus sees your weariness and need for relief.
- He wants to teach you and help you.
- When you turn to him, he will give your soul rest.

THE PROMISE
GOD'S WORK IN YOUR LIFE IS UNSTOPPABLE

Though our bodies are dying, our spirits are being renewed
every day.   2 Corinthians 4:16

T HE physical signs of aging are impossible to deny. Perhaps
wrinkles are appearing, or even spreading and deepening. Or
your hairline is retreating. Certain clothes no longer fit. You
grunt involuntarily when you bend over to tie your shoes or
pick something up.

Fact #1: You are getting older.

Fact #2: Your body is wearing out.

Fact #3: You have two choices: You can devote all your
waking energies to trying—futilely—to preserve your temporal
body. Or you can accept the inevitability of physical aging and
focus your attention instead on what God is doing in you spiritually.

That's what today's promise is talking about. Our physical
bodies are dying a little bit every day. In the life to come, God
will resurrect and renew your body. It'll be the ultimate
makeover. But for now, his focus is on your inner self—on
changing you, maturing you into the person he wants you to be.

Shouldn't that be your primary focus too?

PRAYING GOD'S PROMISE

My body is breaking down. Oh Lord, give me a sense of balance. I want to take care of my body, but I do not want to be like so many in our health- and beauty-obsessed culture who are looking for some kind of nonexistent fountain of youth. You are renewing my spirit every day. Give me joy in the realization that any seemingly "negative" changes in my physical appearance or health can be countered by continual "positive" changes in my spiritual condition.

GOD'S PROMISE TO YOU

- God is constantly changing you from the inside out.

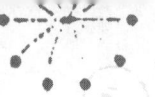
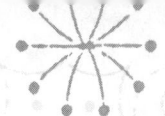

THE PROMISE
GOD SEES EVERYTHING ABOUT YOU

> The Lord sees clearly what a man does, examining every path he takes.
>
> Proverbs 5:21

WOULD you modify your behavior this week if you knew that your every word and deed were going to be videotaped and shown on a big screen to your family, neighbors, or fellow church members? Of course you would! Perhaps even on a grand scale. There's nothing like a little accountability to make people "straighten up and fly right."

What we often tend to forget is that God *does* see everything about us. Today's verse indicates that he knows our thoughts and motives. He monitors our conversations, plans, and behaviors. And one day we will have to stand before the Lord and give an account for the way we have lived (2 Corinthians 5:10).

As you ponder your schedule for the day ahead (or next week or next month or next year), ask yourself, *What do I need to change in light of the fact that I will one day answer to God for the way I chose to live the life he so graciously gave me?*

PRAYING GOD'S PROMISE

God, you see me, and you know me. Nothing about me is hidden from your sight. Lord, what a sobering and convicting thought. Forgive me for the times I have foolishly acted as if you were oblivious to my lifestyle choices. You examine the path I am on. Show me if I need to do an about-face and in what areas of my life. I want my life to bring you pleasure, not embarrassment.

GOD'S PROMISE TO YOU

- God sees what you do.
- He examines your actions.

THE PROMISE
GOD TURNS SORROW INTO JOY

Sing to the Lord, all you godly ones! Praise his holy name. His anger lasts for a moment, but his favor lasts a lifetime! Weeping may go on all night, but joy comes with the morning.

Psalm 30:4-5

WHEN life turns ugly and stays ugly, it's easy to get trapped in an emotional vortex. Trials overwhelm us. Struggles never seem to end. Pain is unceasing. Disappointment, discouragement, disillusionment, devastation, depression—down and down we spin until we may finally believe that God hates us and that all hope is lost.

In Psalm 30 King David gives us a different perspective: the promise that hard times do not last forever. Whether our difficulties are trials intended to strengthen us and test our faith (James 1) or divine discipline intended to correct and train us (2 Corinthians 12), the fact remains that God is worthy of our praise.

We can count on him to shower his people with his favor. Even when we feel as if the night of weeping will never end, God's Word assures us that the morning will surely come, and with it will come joy. Verse 11 of Psalm 30 promises that God will eventually turn your mourning into dancing.

PRAYING GOD'S PROMISE

Lord, you are holy and worthy of praise! I want to worship you at all times—when life is good and when it is difficult. Hard and sad times are temporary, but your favor is continually with me. Give me the maturity, God, to trust you. Though I weep and mourn now, I want to believe—really believe—that you are in control and that better times are ahead.

GOD'S PROMISE TO YOU

- God's favor endures for a lifetime.
- You will not weep forever.
- God will bring you joy.

THE PROMISE
GOD HELPS THE HURTING

All praise to the God and Father of our Lord Jesus Christ. He is the source of every mercy and the God who comforts us. He comforts us in all our troubles so that we can comfort others. When others are troubled, we will be able to give them the same comfort God has given us.   2 Corinthians 1:3-4

WHAT does physical busyness look like? We rush to and fro, trying to do this and that, until we don't know whether we're coming or going.

Now, what does soul busyness look like? Our minds are spinning with worry or fear, and our hearts are heavy with care. Soul busyness explains how you can be on vacation, lying in a hammock with your eyes closed, and still be on the verge of losing it.

What's the prescription for busyness of soul? There is no simple cure. But the promise above is a good tonic. Look at it. God is "the source of every mercy." He is "the God who comforts."

And take note that his comfort is so abundant that after it flows into our anxious lives and does its reassuring work, there's more than enough left to overflow from us into the busy, troubled soul of someone near to us.

PRAYING GOD'S PROMISE

God, you are the source of every mercy. Thank you! I can always turn to you. Keep me from looking to anyone or anything else to meet my deepest needs. You are the God who comforts your children in all their troubles. Always, I find help and peace in you. After I have experienced your comfort, I am to comfort others. Make me a soothing, healing tool in your hand. Grant that I might give help to others as I have been helped.

GOD'S PROMISE TO YOU

- God is the source of every mercy.
- He comforts you in all your troubles.
- After God's comfort flows into you, it flows through you to others who need it.

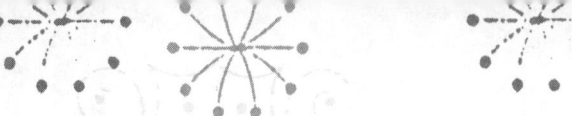

THE PROMISE
GOD IS THE SOURCE OF YOUR WEALTH

> Tell those who are rich in this world not to be proud and not to
> trust in their money, which will soon be gone. But their trust
> should be in the living God, who richly gives us all we need
> for our enjoyment. Tell them to use their money to do good.
> They should be rich in good works and should give generously
> to those in need, always being ready to share with others
> whatever God has given them. 1 Timothy 6:17-18

BEWARE of anyone who says that God promises to give his followers financial prosperity.

First, the Scriptures don't say that. Second, the experiences of millions of faithful believers through the ages don't back up such an extravagant claim. Countless people have served God their whole lives and have lived out their days in abject poverty.

What the Bible does assert is that God owns everything (Psalm 24:1) and that sometimes he chooses to bless certain of his people with great material wealth (Deuteronomy 8:10-18).

For reasons known only to God, those of us in the West have been especially blessed at this time in history. Compared to our brothers and sisters in most other nations, we are rich.

How should we respond to such great blessing? With humility. *God* is the one who gives us the ability to earn and acquire

money and possessions (Deuteronomy 8:18). With grateful hearts we should both enjoy his lavish provision *and* use those resources to continually bless others in need.

PRAYING GOD'S PROMISE

God, I thank you for your material provision. I have so much! I may not make the annual Forbes *list of richest people, but compared to the billions of people worldwide who earn less than five hundred dollars a year, I am fabulously wealthy. You provide money and things for me so that I might enjoy life and use what you've given me to bless others. Keep me, Lord, from being greedy or selfish. Help me to find a God-honoring balance in my stewardship of the resources that you have put in my care. Show me practical and creative ways to use my money to do good. I want to be rich in good works. Lord, make me ever more generous and willing to share your blessings.*

GOD'S PROMISE TO YOU

- Your money will not last forever.
- God gives you all you need for your enjoyment.
- He blesses you so that you can bless others.

THE PROMISE
GOD IS SLOWLY CHANGING YOU

I am sure that God, who began the good work within you, will continue his work until it is finally finished on that day when Christ Jesus comes back again.   Philippians 1:6

BUSYNESS not only rears its head in our personal lives and careers, but it is also evident in our approach to the spiritual life.

Personal quiet times, small-group gatherings, worship services, short-term mission trips, special seminars and conferences, outreach events, prayer meetings, church ministry obligations—the list of "good" activities is long—and exhausting. Some eager-to-grow followers of Christ try to do it all. They attend every church function. They serve on every committee.

Inevitably, though, these well-meaning believers experience deep disappointment. Despite their faithful efforts to change and grow by plunging themselves into a whirlwind of religious activity, they find that they still struggle with sinful desires and old habits. They are learning a crucial lesson: Spiritual busyness is not the way to holiness.

Today's promise says that God will patiently change us in his way and according to his timetable. We can cease our striving and relax. God is at work in us!

PRAYING GOD'S PROMISE

God, I praise you for your great salvation! You not only took away my sin, but you gave me a new nature that longs to please you. I thank you for not giving up on me—for working in my heart, day in and day out, to make me like Christ. Continue your work, Lord. Mold me and make me into the image of Christ. I look forward to the day when your work in me is complete. Though my progress is slow and I often seem to be so far from what you want me to be, I know that your plan cannot be thwarted. Praise you, Father!

GOD'S PROMISE TO YOU

- God has begun a good work in you.
- He will continue his good work in you.
- He will complete his good work in you.

THE PROMISE
GOD IS CONCERNED THAT YOU NOT BURN OUT

Jesus said, "Let's get away from the crowds for a while and rest." There were so many people coming and going that Jesus and his apostles didn't even have time to eat.　　　Mark 6:31

THE King James Version of the Bible translates Jesus' statement above as "Come . . . apart . . . and rest," which prompted some wise guy to quip, "Jesus is saying here that if we don't come apart *and rest,* we'll eventually just come apart!"

Now you may chuckle at that, but that's the idea behind today's verse! God has built a work-rest-work-rest rhythm into the very fabric of life. The prime example of this is in Genesis 2:1-3, where we read that after God completed his work of creation, he rested on the seventh day and set it aside as a day to rest. When we violate this natural order of things by nonstop busyness and excessive work or ministry involvement, we soon burn out. No wonder Jesus deliberately scheduled retreats for himself (Matthew 14:13) and his disciples—intentional trips into quiet or remote places.

What about you? How long has it been since you really ceased your busyness and rested? God promises to give you rest, and if you're seriously empty inside, he may even want you to take some extended time off from some of your responsibilities.

PRAYING GOD'S PROMISE

Lord, when I feel drained physically, emotionally, and spiritually, give me the wisdom to recognize the warning signs of burnout. Forgive my failure to seek regular rest and replenishment. I can't be effective for you if I am running on empty. I want the rest that you offer. God, please restore me. Help me to realize that it's not a sin to relax. Grant me renewed vigor and excitement for both work and ministry. Make me willing to do whatever I need to do to develop a healthy balance between activity and rest.

GOD'S PROMISE TO YOU

- If you will pull away from your busy schedule, God will give you the rest you need.

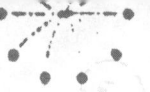
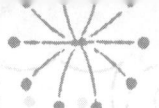

THE PROMISE
GOD FORGIVES THE SIN OF BUSYNESS

If we confess our sins to him, he is faithful and just to forgive us and to cleanse us from every wrong. 1 John 1:9

SOMETIMES it hits like a lightning bolt. At other times it comes gradually, as if we are waking up from a deep slumber.

"It" is the sense that our lives are out of balance. We see ourselves as we truly are: frantic people, rushing through our days, trying so feverishly to have it all and do it all. We realize that all we have to show for our busyness is frustration and exhaustion. We experience feelings of regret because we see, again, that whenever we choose a life jammed with nonstop activity, we are also choosing to shut the door on life's greatest treasures—intimacy with God and deep relationships with the people in our lives.

Regret is not a fun place to be. But it *is* the first step to a new and better way of living. It is only when we face up to our wrong priorities and foolish choices and admit them to God that we find cleansing and forgiveness and the hope to try again.

PRAYING GOD'S PROMISE

God, I praise you because you are faithful and just. Thank you for never giving up on me. I know that you will deal with me gently and fairly. I admit my failure to live the simple life you desire for me. I have sinned in my busyness. I agree with you that my priorities and actions have been wrong, but I also know that you have forgiven me! Thank you for your promise to wipe away my sin and to cleanse me completely. Lord, it is wonderful to be right with you, to be clean. Give me the grace I need today to avoid making the same foolish choices again.

GOD'S PROMISE TO YOU

- God is faithful.
- He is just.
- He will forgive you and cleanse you when you confess your sins to him.

TOPICAL INDEX

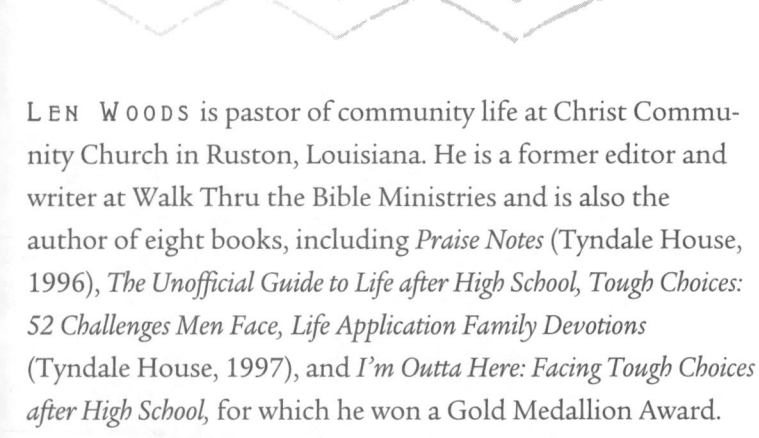

LEN WOODS is pastor of community life at Christ Community Church in Ruston, Louisiana. He is a former editor and writer at Walk Thru the Bible Ministries and is also the author of eight books, including *Praise Notes* (Tyndale House, 1996), *The Unofficial Guide to Life after High School, Tough Choices: 52 Challenges Men Face, Life Application Family Devotions* (Tyndale House, 1997), and *I'm Outta Here: Facing Tough Choices after High School,* for which he won a Gold Medallion Award. He also contributed to the *Life Application Bible for Students* as well as the *Parents Resource Bible* and the *Praise and Worship Study Bible,* all published by Tyndale House.

Len dreams of one day making a hole in one, visiting the Holy Land, seeing the New Orleans Saints win the Super Bowl, and writing a best-selling novel—not necessarily in that order. Len and his wife have two sons and live in Ruston.

PRAYING GOD'S PROMISES SERIES